WARBIRI
S E R

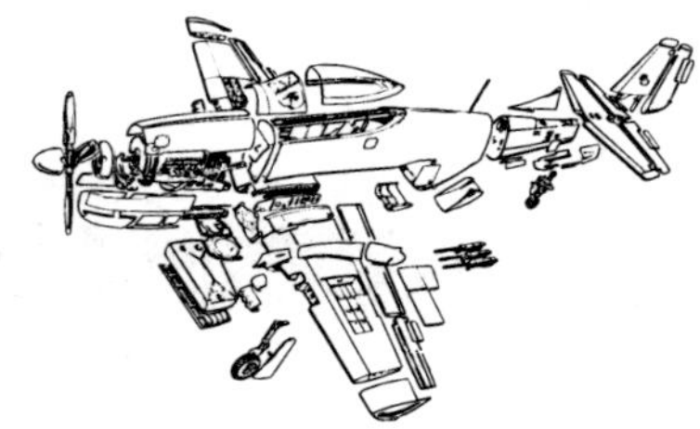

VOLUME 38

LOCKHEED F-104 STARFIGHTER

BY JIM UPTON

specialty press
PUBLISHERS AND WHOLESALERS

Published by
Specialty Press Publishers and Wholesalers
39966 Grand Avenue
North Branch, MN 55056
United States of America
(800) 895-4585 or (651) 277-1400
http://www.specialtypress.com

ISBN 978-1-58007-187-1

Front Cover: *A clean-configuration Lockheed F-104C Starfighter, USAF 56-883 (msn 1171) climbs steeply. The ability to accelerate in combat, either to close in for attack, intercept an intruder quickly, or to evade an attacker, is an indispensable requirement for an air superiority fighter. The F-104 can accelerate while climbing from subsonic speeds to Mach 2 in less than three minutes.* (Lockheed Martin)
Back Cover (Left Top): *A dramatic view of NASA 826 in 1990 over the Mojave Desert near Edwards AFB. An in-flight experiment pod is mounted on the bottom of the fuselage and an air data instrumentation pod is on the right wing pylon.* (NASA)
Back Cover (Right Top): *Inboard profile of an experimental escape capsule shows its major components.* (Lockheed via Pete Clukey)
Back Cover (Right Lower): *Rocket motor in the NF-104 was a Rocketdyne AR2-3 that produced 6,000 pounds of thrust. The rocket motor burned the same JP-4 fuel as the F-104 along with a hydrogen peroxide oxidizer. Lockheed test pilot Jack Woodman performs preflight. Notice the longer wings in this view.* (Lockheed, Dave Steinbacher collection)
Title Page: *A USAF F-104A and a German F-104G fly in formation over the Mojave Desert, providing an excellent comparison of the different vertical stabilizers.* (AFFTC History Office via Tony Landis)

WARBIRDTECH SERIES

TABLE OF CONTENTS

LOCKHEED F-104 STARFIGHTER

FOREWORD

BY DICK HEPPE

To this day in January of 2003, I recall a snowy night in December of 1952 when aboard a TWA Constellation, Kelly Johnson, Bill Ralston, and I flew into Dayton to present the Air Force our ideas about a new superiority fighter. Kelly needs no introduction; Ralston was to become the Project Engineer on the XF-104 program; and I was the project aerodynamicist - the guy who was supposed to make sure the darn thing would fly.

The concept was based on needs growing out of the Korean War and was to be higher and faster than anything else around. Chuck Yeager had only broken the sound barrier on rocket power in 1947, and much of the industry was struggling just to reach Mach 2 with research aircraft. But here we were, proposing to fly in one year a fully operational combat Mach 2 fighter. I guess we were pretty bold!

When we went home at the end of the week we were so encouraged that we pulled out all the stops and, sure enough, a contract followed in March of 1953. A year later in 1954 we made first flight, and after a complete redesign to accommodate a different engine, went operational with the first squadron in 1958 - about five years after the Dayton visit. Little did we realize at the time that we were setting forces in motion that would result in the production of more than 2,500 aircraft in the largest international military aircraft production program in the history of the world!

In this book, Jim Upton, who was one of Lockheed's finest professional flight test engineers and lived on the flight line with many of Lockheed's best aircraft over the years, has done a magnificent job of telling you the story of this fantastic project. He has assembled a world of valuable facts and has put just the right set of observations on how and who did it all. You will learn everything worth knowing about the F-104 in this book.

Dick Heppe stayed deeply involved in the conception and development of every Burbank airplane from the XF-90 to the F-22 for a period of more than 40 years. He was a significant part of the original design team on the F-104, progressing though a number of management positions, and in 1984 he became President of the Lockheed-California Company. (Lockheed Martin)

Dick Heppe,
Retired President,
Lockheed-California Company
2003

PREFACE

AND ACKNOWLEDGEMENTS

It was the aerial combat against soviet-built Mig-15s during the Korean War that indicated the United States needed a new jet fighter to succeed the Lockheed F-80 Shooting Star and the North American F-86 Sabre.

Among the designs considered for this purpose was one created by Clarence L. "Kelly" Johnson and his engineering group at Lockheed-California Company. In early 1953 the United States Air Force accepted this proposal and the F-104 Starfighter was born. For his design work on the aircraft, Johnson received the prestigious Collier Trophy in 1959 from the American Institute of Aeronautics and Astronautics.

Five to 10 years ahead of its time when the first prototype F-104 took off in March 1954, the F-104 was truly a pioneering effort. It was the world's first Mach 2 production jet, and it rewrote the performance books for speed, altitude, and time to climb. Aircraft enthusiasts called it "the missile with a man in it."

The Starfighter also generated the greatest international cooperative venture in the history of the aerospace industry. Its appearance coincided with the established needs of West German, Netherlands, Belgian and Italian air forces for a NATO weapons system to help them fulfill their role in the defense of Europe. The F-104's spectacular performance ultimately led to licensed production agreements with Canada, Japan, and the four European nations.

Before its production run ended in 1979, the F-104 had become the most widely used Mach 2 fighter ever developed. A total of 2,578 Starfighters were built by manufacturers in seven countries. In 2003 Italy is still flying its updated F-104S model Starfighters.

WHAT YOU WILL FIND HERE

This book's chapters are laid out more or less chronologically. Starting with preliminary design, you will get some insight into the designers' role and responsibilities, followed by details and descriptions of the Starfighter's features and systems. You will also hear flight testers' F-104 recollections about wild rides through gun problems. Eighteen models of the F-104 are described and supported by photos of each model.

The Starfighter's weapons were very advanced for their time, with the first airborne 6,000-rounds-a-minute Gatling gun, bombing systems that allowed the pilot to attack a target that could not be seen, a semi-automatic bombing technique that could deliver a nuclear weapon at high speed and perform an escape maneuver, and a gun sight system that enabled a pilot to track targets without a visual reference, as in a dark night.

Starfighters Worldwide describes, with photos of each, the 14 countries that had the F-104. Modifications to the 104 range from NASA

Lockheed always had a number of irons in the fire at the same time. Two of Kelly Johnson's products made their first flights in 1956 and 1957; the YF-104A Starfighter on 17 February 1956 and the CL-329 JetStar on 4 September 1957. The JetStar was built in 241 days. First flight crew on the JetStar included Kelly Johnson on the right, and (right to left) flight test engineer Ernie Joiner and test pilots Ray Goudey and Bob Shumacher. (Lockheed, Jim Upton Collection)

View of Lockheed Burbank in 1956. First flights of the YF-104A Starfighter and CL-329 JetStar were taking place at Palmdale and Edwards Air Force Base at that time. The Lockheed plants completely surrounded the Burbank airport. P2V Neptunes, and both military and civil Constellations were on the flight lines. Today, all but the airport are gone, with a huge shopping mall now filling the location of the B-1 plant, which is off the photo to the lower right. (Lockheed, Jim Upton Collection)

test modification to support space programs to the rocket-powered NF-104A Aerospace trainer. Several little-known programs that were classified at the time are described here with photos. This book also covers civil use of the Starfighter from NASA use to a private venture that captured the Low Altitude World Speed Record that still stands today.

AND MY THANKS TO ALL

The help of many friends makes a publication like this possible. You were there when needed to answer my questions, and I truly thank you. I especially want to acknowledge the following contributors: Dave Steinbacher and Tony Landis for lending your extensive selection of photos. Denny Lombard and Ellen Bendell at Lockheed Martin, Pete Clukey, Bill Norton, Jim Fitzgerald, Frank Brown, Phil Sullivan, Mel Cassidy, John Peterson, Ken Pittman, John Whittenbury, Tom Laughlin, Bill Nickloff, Chuck Schisler, Joe Carrillo, Dave Gill, Dick Fetty, Chuck Price, Art Troutman, Dave Kerzie, Franz Enzinger, Ed Shadle, George Wiltsey, Nelson Harnois, Frank Wyche, Bill Taschek, Ernie Joiner, Ray Goudey, Henry Combs, Mark Sherman, Dan O'Hara, and Chuck Sammons. Dick Heppe for your review, helpful comments, and your time to write the Foreword; and to my wife Carol for your editing and supportive patience.

Jim Upton
February 2003

Origin of the F-104

1

Design, Development, and Manufacturing

In the 1949-1950 period, Lockheed Aircraft Corporation had been awarded a contract together with Convair for Weapon System MX 1179. It was to be the ultimate 1954 Interceptor, and it finally emerged as the F-102. It was about this time that "Korea" took place, prompting the Air Force to switch Lockheed to a Day Superiority Fighter, designed especially for Korean War type operation. Design evaluation started immediately for a day fighter that was to have superior performance. Existing specifications and airplane requirements were to be disregarded if they penalized performance.

Clarence L. "Kelly" Johnson was Lockheed vice-president of engineering and research, creator of a number of Lockheed aircraft designs including the P-38 Lightning and the first production U.S. jet aircraft, the P-80 Shooting Star.

Johnson went to Korea in 1951 to see first-hand how our fighters were performing and what was needed in a fighter aircraft. The battlefield tour included Lt. General Benjamin Chidlaw, chief of Material Command, other Air Force officers, and Lee Atwood, vice president of engineering for North American Aviation (builder of the P-51 and F-86). The

The second XF-104, USAF s/n 53-7787, on the Edwards North Base lakebed. By this time, the National insignia had been moved to the fuselage forward of the wing. First flight on the number two XF occurred on 6 October 1954. (Lockheed, Dave Steinbacher collection)

Lockheed XF-104 USAF s/n 53-7786 was the first of two prototypes. It is shown here at the restricted North Base area of Edwards Air Force Base in early 1954. First flight occurred on 4 March 1954. (Lockheed, Dave Steinbacher collection)

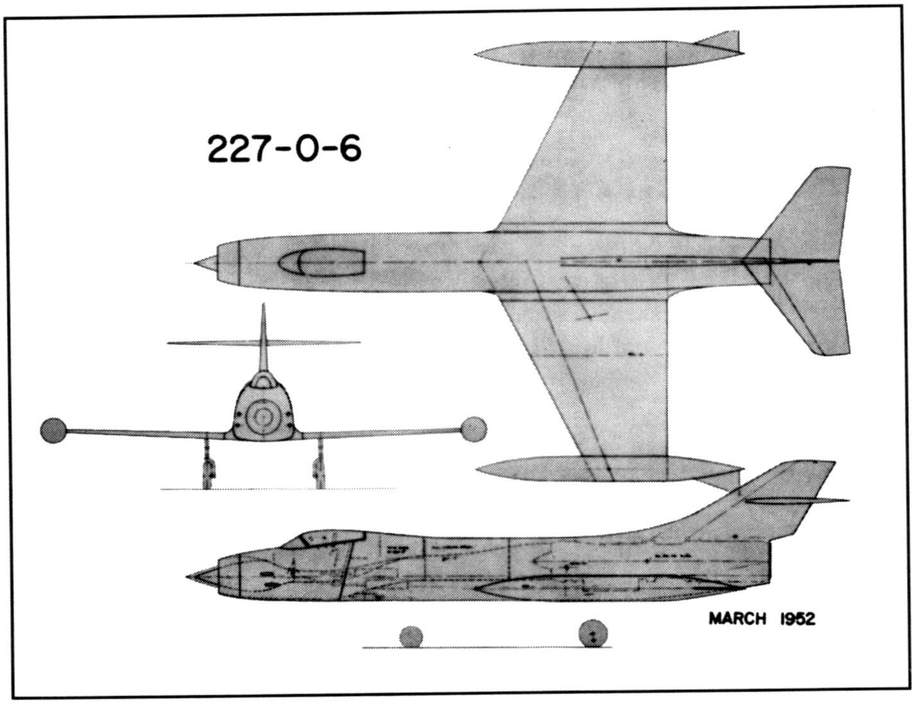

Preliminary design number CL-227-0-6 illustrates one of the early attempts to design the new interceptor. It used a nose inlet similar to the F-86 Sabre. The inlet provided variable area by moving the cone fore and aft. (Lockheed Martin)

Air Force wanted to find out what our fighter pilots needed, and they wanted the aircraft designers to know so they would be able to meet these needs in their designs. This was the first war where both sides were using jet aircraft. North Korean/Chinese MiG 15s fought against South Korean/USAF F-80s, F-84s, and later F-86s.

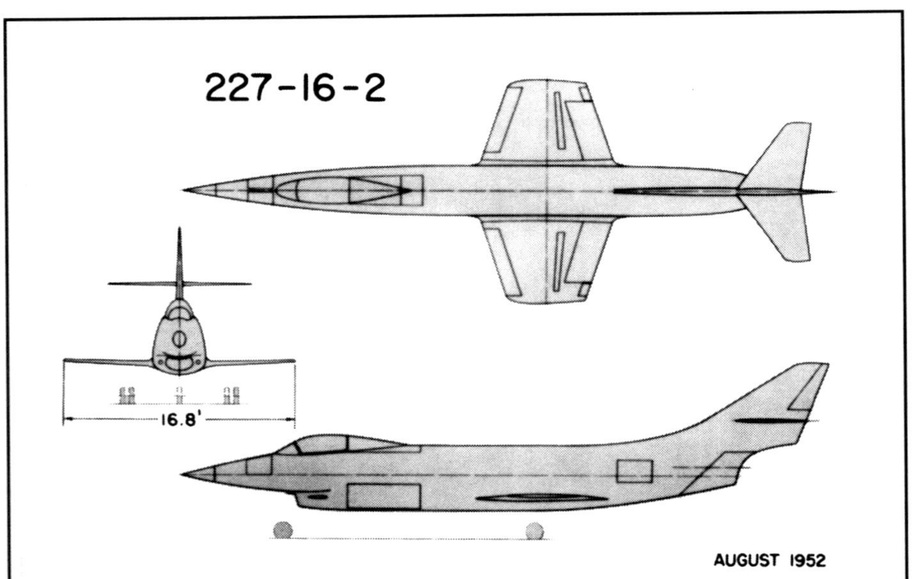

Preliminary design CL-227-16-2 was a trend step in the right direction. This was a small fighter weighing about 8,000 pounds. It was on this design that the thickness of the F-104 wing was determined. Wind tunnel personnel ran tests on this type of wing and it became standard for all of the subsequent models. (Lockheed Martin)

Speed and Altitude

The reply was unanimous. United States Air Force fighter pilots wanted speed and altitude. When Kelly Johnson returned to the United States, he started the process to design a jet fighter that would fly higher and faster than anything flying anywhere. At this point there was no formal USAF requirement.

Design Steps to the F-104

A small group of engineers was assigned the task of establishing the preliminary design for the F-104. This group included Bill Ralston, Ken Pittman, Dick Heppe, Harry Drell, Jim Pray, Dick Boehme, and Don Perry.

Preliminary Design Phase

During preliminary design operation, many variations in aircraft type were considered, and more than 100 different types were tried and rejected. Some of the major steps follow. The dates shown on the illustrations, though not accurate by month, are accurately presented in order of design steps.

Preliminary design number CL-227-0-6 illustrates one of the early attempts to design the new interceptor. It used a nose inlet similar to the Sabre. The inlet provided variable area by moving the cone fore and aft. As in all the early designs, the aircraft had a low wing, which was thought to be easier to build as it provided a place to pivot the landing gear.

Preliminary design CL-227-16-2 was a step in the right direction. It was a small fighter weighing about

8,000 pounds. The nose and main gear wheels and tires were all identical. The wheels folded into the fuselage and the oleo fit into the very thin wing by using a dual strut landing gear with one oleo located behind the other. It was on this design that the thickness of the F-104 wing was determined. The wing thickness matched this new gear design. After wind tunnel personnel ran tests on this wing type it became standard for all of the subsequent models.

CL-227-0-11 appears to be quite a radical departure, but it is significant because it is the real ancestor to the F-104 airplane as it is today. Many of the principle features can be traced to this design. The symmetrical fuselage was used because it looked good. However, wind tunnel tests proved that for supersonic flight the mid-wing had less drag than other types. The new landing gear — pivoting from the fuselage and folding forward — was first tried on this design. The flush cockpit, however, didn't work out too well, and it became necessary to grow a canopy on the airplane. The delta wing, which was in vogue at that time, didn't work out either because at higher speed ranges it had more drag than a simple straight wing.

Preliminary design CL-227-8-1 reflects a continuing favor for that the delta wing, and in order to get proper performance the aircraft started to grow. This version had a gross weight of approximately 30,000 pounds.

Assembly of Building Blocks

About this time the designers were becoming fairly objective in grouping components together. They made "paper dolls" of each major component, including pitot tube, radar, cockpit, electronic equipment,

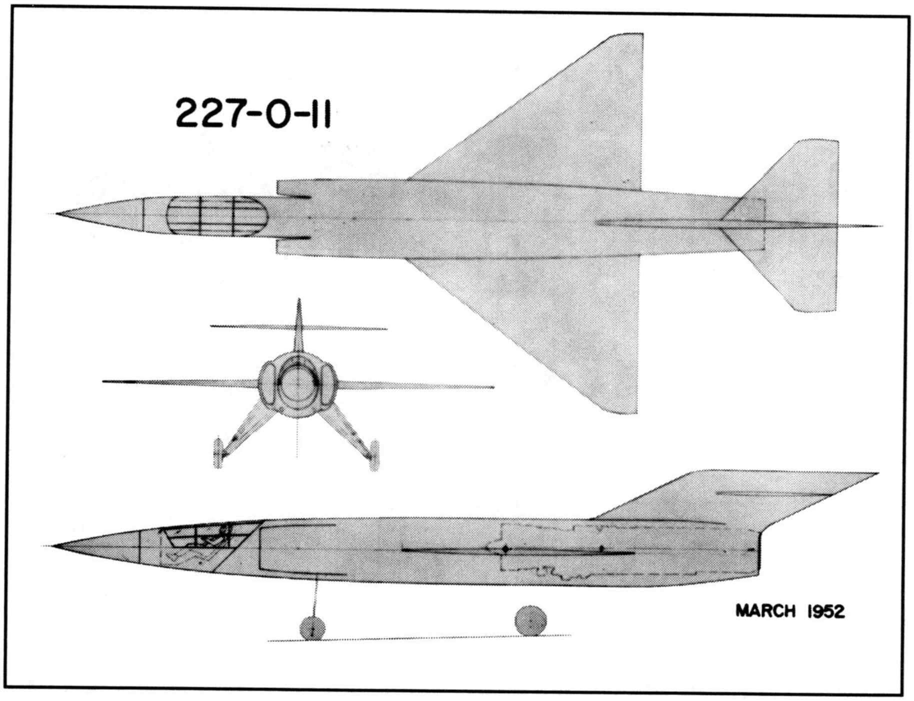

CL-227-0-11 appears to be quite a radical departure; it is, however, a significant design because this is the real ancestor to the F-104 airplane as it is today. Wind tunnel tests proved that for supersonic flight the mid-wing had less drag than other types. The flush cockpit, however, didn't work out too well and it was necessary to grow a canopy on the airplane. (Lockheed Martin)

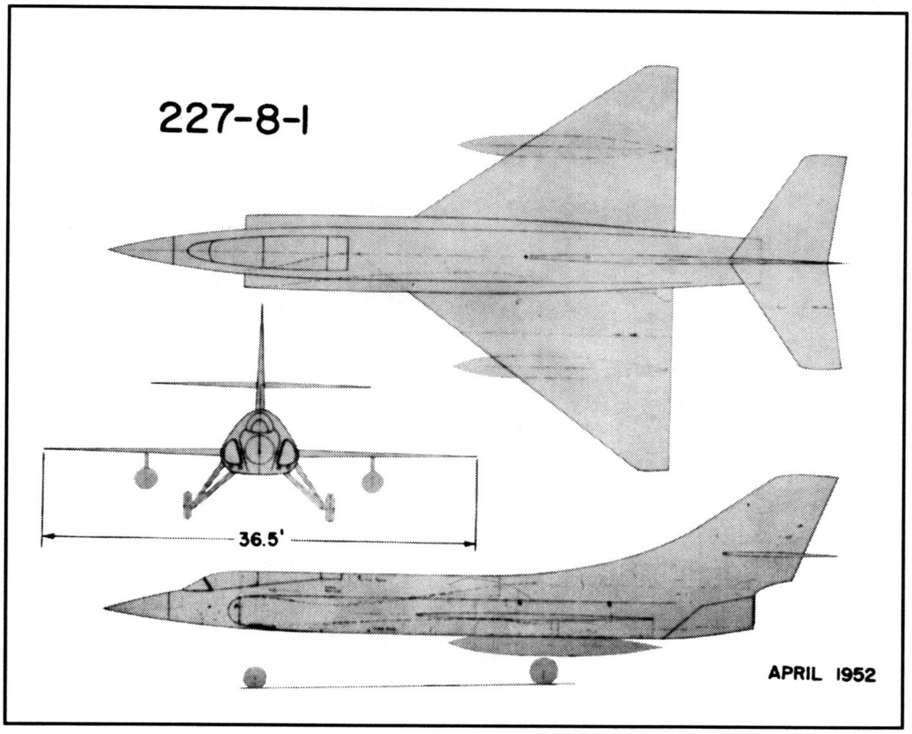

CL-227-8-1 shows that the delta wing was still favored, and in order to get proper performance the airplane started to grow. (Lockheed Martin)

F-104 building blocks were used in evaluating design effects of location of key components. This was done by making "paper dolls" of each major component, making it easy to move the component around until a suitable location was found. (Lockheed Martin)

electrical load center, refrigeration equipment, the engine air inlets, landing gear, gun and ammunition, fuel tanks and power plant.

The illustration at the top of this page illustrates the method used to assemble these components. First, the only satisfactory location for a pitot tube in a high supersonic aircraft is out ahead of everything else, even taking priority over the radar. Designers had to find a means of making the radar work by looking around the pitot tube. Next was the pilot's cockpit, with electrical load center and the gun, which had to face forward. These components were put together in this fashion to form the forward portion of the fuselage. Next, all of the components that didn't have to face forward were hidden behind the cockpit section. Hidden components included the refrigeration system, electronic equipment, nose gear and ammunition can. These formed the section that followed the cockpit, and remaining components were then added. The engine air ducts were added, which had to have a clear view looking forward, then the main fuel tanks, main landing gear, and then the engine. All of these components were combined to form the fuselage mid-section and aft section. The result provided the most efficient cross sectional area with maximum airplane utility.

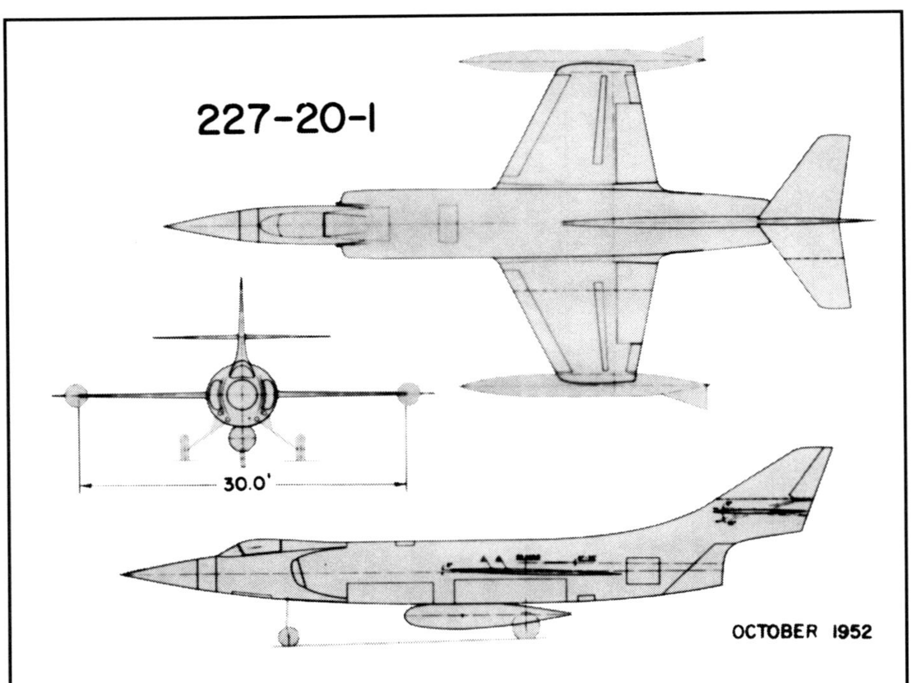

Preliminary design number CL-227-20-1 reflects designers' efforts to reduce size and weight. (Lockheed Martin)

Getting Out Of Hand

Things could get out of hand. In order to get more range and performance it was necessary to add more fuel, which in turn required more structure, which in turn required more fuel. As a result, the designers found themselves on a vicious merry-go-round in which the aircraft's weight increased rapidly with little improvement in performance. At one point, take-off weight reached around 50,000 pounds.

Preliminary design CL-227-20-1 reflects efforts to reduce the craft's size and weight. By selecting a smaller engine and making other design economies, designers cut the weight in half to around 25,000 pounds without affecting the desired range and high-speed performance. It was decided that the size could be reduced further.

A smaller aircraft, preliminary design CL-242-19-1, followed in an attempt to further cut in the weight and size and still maintain the required performance. But at an empty weight of 9,000 pounds, this design did not work out. It was provided with a new V windshield and had a low tail configuration, which designers believed had many advantages. But it turned out there were more disadvantages to the low tail, and it was abandoned.

Preliminary design CL-242-23-1 illustrates an attempt to reduce the frontal area of the aircraft by hiding fuel and landing gear behind the air scoops. As it worked out this was a pretty good transonic aircraft but performance was unsatisfactory at higher speeds.

The upper part of CL-242-1-27 (on the following page) represents a study to determine whether there was any advantage to installing the landing gear inside of a wing pod. This study permitted a reduction in the length of the fuselage; however, it would also have eliminated capability for future growth in carrying armament stores, etc. The decrease in length also increased the drag due to a less favorable ratio of cross sectional area to the length.

The lower drawing is actually very close to the design finally selected. It weighed about 12,000 pounds empty.

Preliminary design CL-246-1-1 was almost the final configuration, but designers still found it necessary to make a few changes. The "V" windshield had to be altered because the gun-sight would not work properly through anything but a flat glass. The scoops were changed to improve their efficiency,

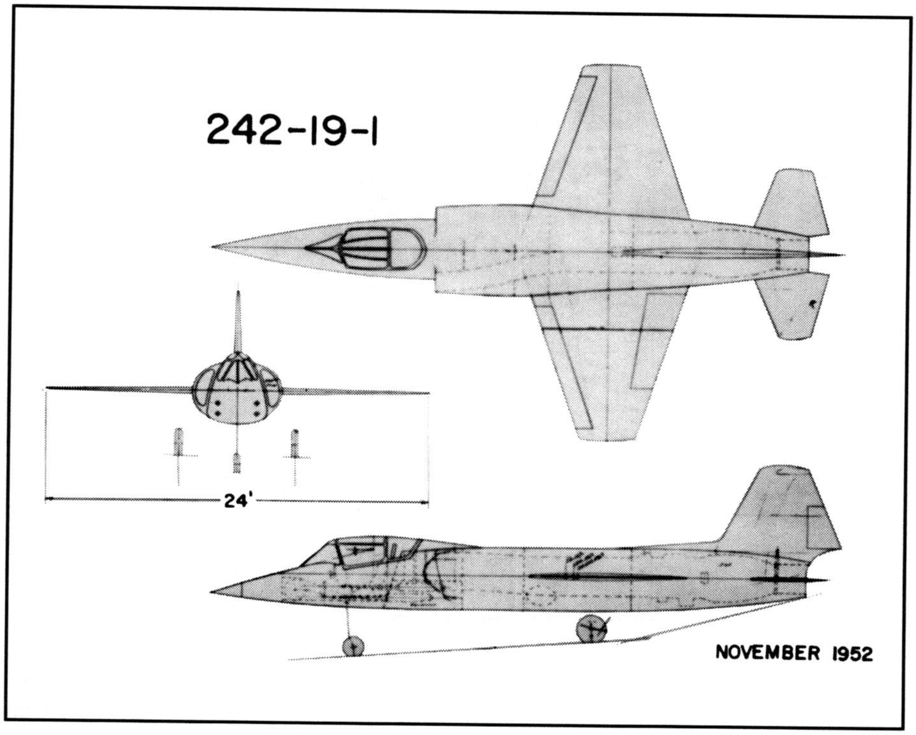

Preliminary design number CL-242-19-1 was an additional attempt to cut weight and size. While the weight was reduced, the low tail configuration did not work out. (Lockheed Martin)

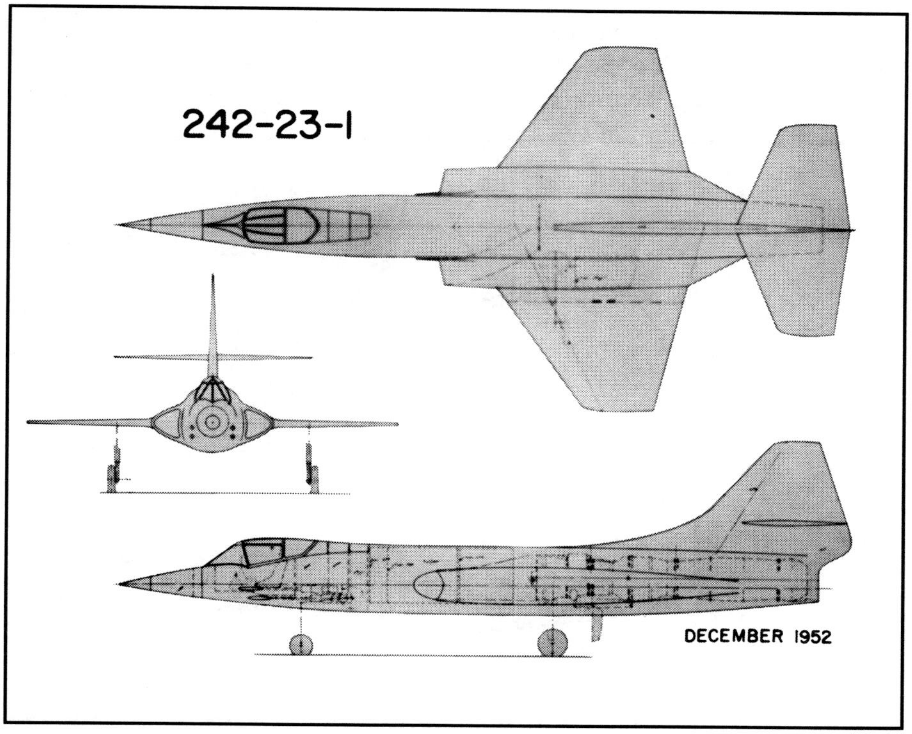

Preliminary design number CL-224-23-1 illustrates an attempt to reduce the frontal area of the airplane by hiding fuel and landing gear behind the air scoops. (Lockheed Martin)

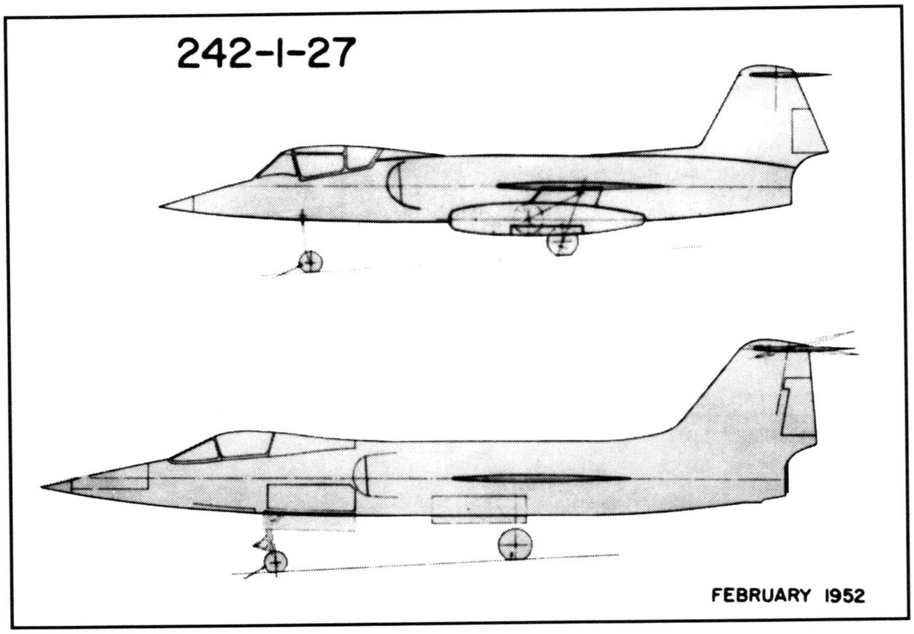

The upper drawing in CL-242-1-27 represents a study to determine whether there was an advantage to installing the landing gear inside of a wing pod. The lower drawing is actually very close to the design that was finally selected. It weighed about 12,000 pounds empty. (Lockheed Martin)

and the horizontal tail was moved to the top of the vertical fin to eliminate inertia coupling. This made the vertical fin so effective that it began to act like a wing during rolling turns. A negative dihedral in the wings was necessary to offset this stabilizing affect.

When the "Area Rule" or "Coke Bottle" effect were considered, designers found that this configuration did fit into the "Area Rule" concept. This dictated that total displacement of the airplane cross section as it progressed from nose to tail would have no humps, which would contribute high-speed drag. Notice that the cross-sectional area increases for the windshield and canopy and then starts to taper off as the air scoops pick up area, resulting in a smooth gradient increase in the cross sectional area to where the wing starts. At this point the scoops begin to reduce and the over-all result is a smooth curve, nose to tail. This is fairly significant in that the "Area Rule" had been followed without pinching the fuselage to obtain the "Coke Bottle" effect. Without it, this could have caused detrimental effects during cruise speeds.

Preliminary Design Complete

The final result of the extensive preliminary design studies for a fighter that would go faster and higher than any aircraft in current use was Lockheed model L-246, which was given Lockheed management approval on 31 October 1952.

Kelly Johnson; Bill Ralston, project leader; and Dick Heppe, aerodynamicist; made a trip to Wright-Patterson Air Force Base in Dayton Ohio in December 1952 to brief the Air Force technical people on the Lockheed L-246 design for a new supersonic fighter. Following this briefing, Kelly went on to the Pentagon in Washington D.C.

Kelly Johnson shared his proposal with General Don Putt, General Don Yates, and Colonel Holloway, who were very receptive. At this point there was no document specifying what the next fighter should be. Colonel Holloway remedied this, telling Kelly to come back in a few hours. Colonel Holloway wrote a

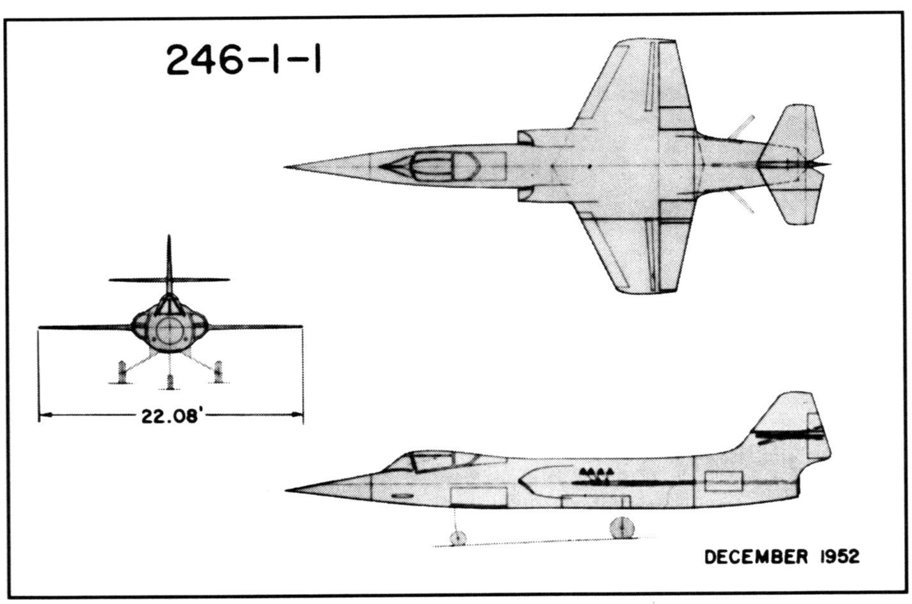

CL-246-1-1 is almost the final configuration, with only a few changes still necessary. The scoops were changed to improve their efficiency, and the horizontal tail was moved to the top of the vertical fin to eliminate inertia coupling. (Lockheed Martin)

page and a quarter on what the USAF required for its next fighting plane. Requirements included that it be lightweight, have certain performance at sea level and high altitude (classified at the time), and carry specific armament, radios, and instrumentation. Colonel Holloway obtained approval from the appropriate generals, and he gave Kelly the requirements and told him to go see what he could do with them.

United States Air Force letter approval for the L-246 design was given to Lockheed in January 1953, followed by a contract to build two XF-104 prototypes on 1 March 1953. Lockheed had started work on its own funds prior to 1 March, including completing wind tunnel tests verifying the L-246 design and development of the shop manufacturing drawings. Total time from contract award to first flight of the XF-104 was only one year — an amazingly short span for building a very advanced aircraft that would fly higher and faster than any existing aircraft.

X-7 Contribution

The very thin, short wing on the F-104 design was a radically new concept that needed early data. Skunk Works engineer Irv Culver was Chief Designer on the X-7. A contract was won to build a vehicle with the purpose of developing a flying test bed for several ramjet engines, capable of self-sustained flight between Mach numbers of 1.7 and 3.0 and at altitudes from sea level to 80,000 feet. These parameters covered the speeds and altitudes the F-104 would be flying. The X-7 was first launched from under the wing of a Boeing B-29 on 7 May 1952, flown by Lockheed test pilot James F. White. It had short stubby wings like the F-104 and had a 105,000-pound-thrust booster rocket that would accelerate the X-7 to supersonic speeds. The booster rocket assembly had large vertical and horizontal stabilizers, and the booster would separate from the X-7 after burnout at supersonic speed and the ram jet engine would take over. In addition to the primary purpose as a ramjet test bed, the X-7 provided valuable data for the F-104. Included were aerodynamic, structural and flutter data. A total of 61 Lockheed X-7s were produced. By the 130th flight in 1960 the X-7 broke all speed and altitude records for air breathing vehicles, reaching Mach 4.31 and 106,000 feet.

The Lockheed Missiles and Space Company (LMSC) X-7 ramjet played a significant part in providing valuable design data for the F-104. The wing profile similarity to the F-104 wing is obvious in this photo of an X-7 mounted on a pole at the Air Force Missile Development Center in Alamogordo New Mexico. (Lockheed Martin)

Number one XF-104 in flight near Edwards Air Force Base. The XF-104 had a different engine (Wright XJ65) and different inlets compared to the F-104A. The "XF" model was also shorter than the "A" model and subsequent 104 models. (Lockheed, Chuck Schisler collection)

An LMSC X-7 ramjet in flight after being dropped by a Boeing B-29. This secret program started with a first flight on 7 May 1952. The ramjet-powered X-7 was boosted to supersonic speed by a 105,000-pound-thrust rocket motor with large vertical and horizontal stabilizers. After rocket burnout, the rocket and stabilizer assembly would separate and the X-7 ramjet engine would take over. (Lockheed Martin)

HVAR Rocket Testing

Since no other aircraft were flying at the speeds the 104 would fly at, there were still many unanswered questions about the design, particularly in the flutter and aeroelastic areas. Five-inch High Velocity Aircraft Rockets (HVAR), which are normally weapons, were also used for obtaining needed data on the F-104 wing and tail design. About 400 HVAR rockets were used, modified to carry wing and tail assemblies and carrying a gun camera on the rocket nose pointed back at the model airfoils to obtain the data, returning the camera to earth by parachute.

Aircraft Description

The Lockheed XF-104 aircraft that emerged is shown at the top of this page. From the time detail design work began the aircraft was built and first flown within one year!

The production F-104 had improvements over the original XF-104 in that it had a General Electric J79 engine in place of the Wright J65 on the XF-104. It also had a longer fuselage to accommodate the larger engine and additional fuel. In addition it had an AC electrical system replacing the DC system, and a Search and Track Radar System together with improved armament capability. Performance was higher with the J79 engine.

The over-all length of the F-104 is 55 feet, with a wingspan of 22 feet. The aircraft's empty weight varies among specific models. The wing area is 196 square feet including that part enclosed within the fuselage. The wing has a very low aspect ratio and is very thin. This wing is believed to be the thinnest ever used on a production aircraft.

The two-place F-104 is similar to the single-place Starfighter. It has

EXTRA

THE LOCKHEED Star

F-104A Unveiled

Newspapermen, Newsreelmen, Magazine Writers, and Photographers as They Took First Look at Starfighter at Palmdale Press Show Yesterday

Two-place F-104D, Lockheed s/n 5043, on the Palmdale flight line. During preflight activities, the temporary cover over the cockpits kept the crew compartment cool in the desert sun where temperatures could reach 125 degrees in the shade. (Lockheed Martin)

Special eight-page edition of the Lockheed Star on 17 April 1956 revealed the first public photos, two years after the first flight of the XF-104. (Jim Upton collection)

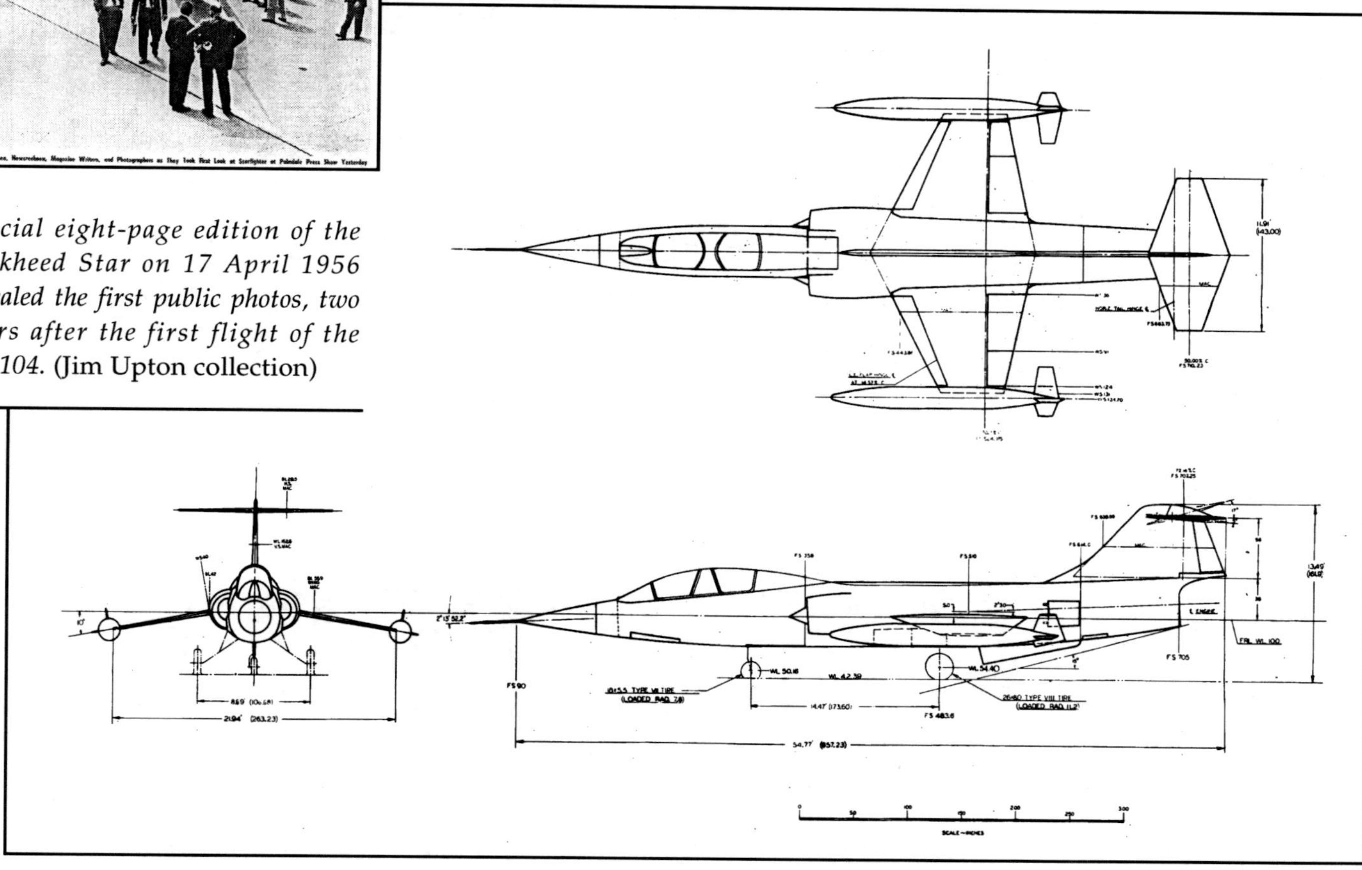

Three-view and specifications for the two-place TF-104G. (Lockheed, Dave Steinbacher collection)

Final design configuration resulted in the XF-104 shown here during a test flight. (Lockheed, Dave Steinbacher collection)

the same overall length and wing spar. The only difference is the addition of a second cockpit identical to the first cockpit. The extra cockpit space made it necessary to reduce the amount of electronic equipment carried. The nose landing gear was changed to retract aft instead of forward, and the fuel capacity was reduced. But the two-place model is just as fast as the single-place airplane; its range, however, is somewhat reduced and it carries less armament.

Production Assembly

The Starfighter was designed for production rates of up to 20 airplanes per day from a single assembly line (see drawing on page 19). Everything was designed to come apart easily. The wings were attached with only ten bolts plus a fairing. The principal fuselage sections were the forward portion and the mid-section, which were split on the vertical centerline. They were completely assembled on the half shell. All equipment, including

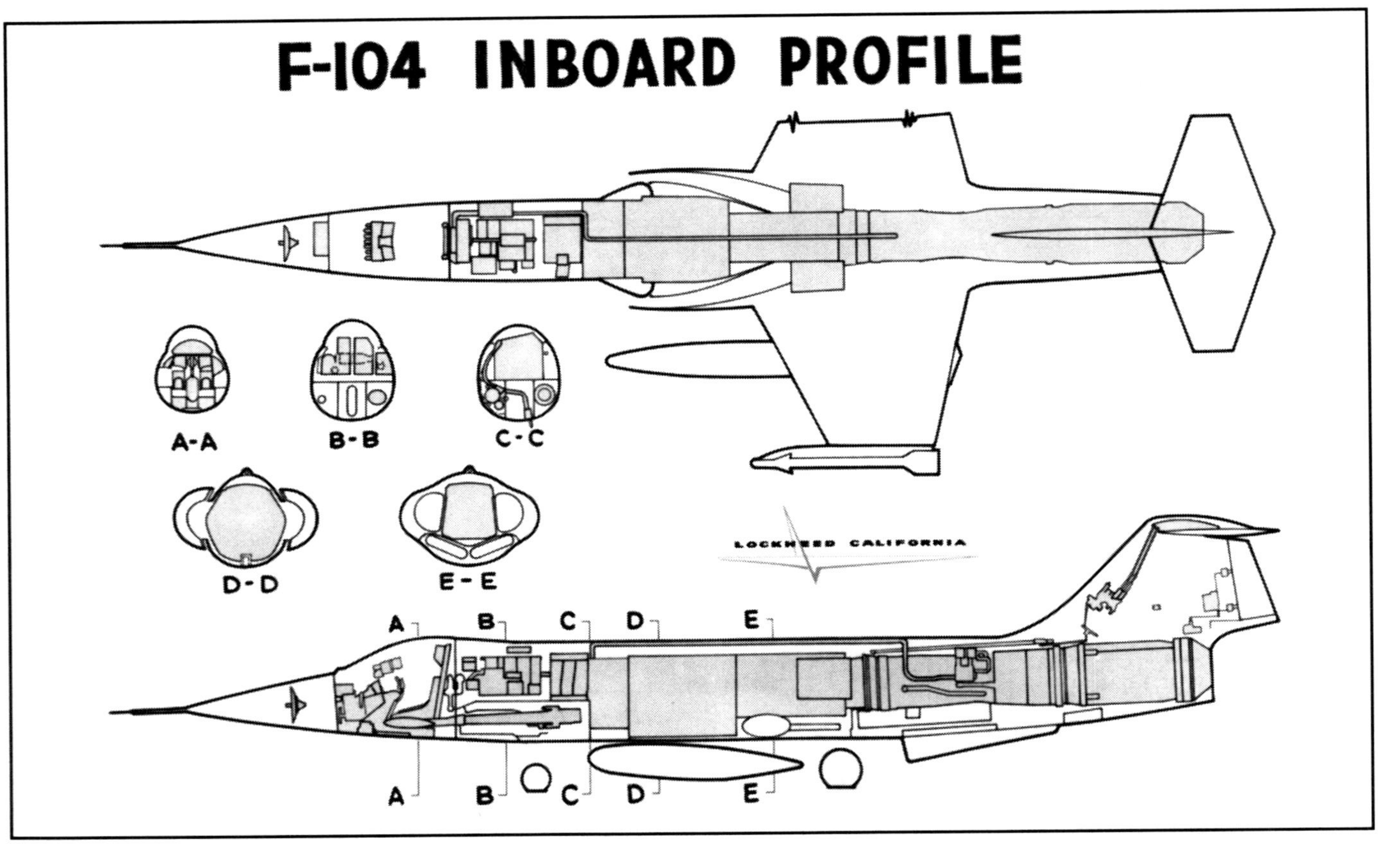

Inboard profile of the single-place Starfighter. Locations of main equipment items are illustrated. First is the radar system, followed by the cockpit, the electronic compartment (which is pressurized to permit high altitude operation), the gun and ammunition, nose landing gear, and electrical load center. This is followed by the fuel tanks and, last, the engine. (Lockheed Martin)

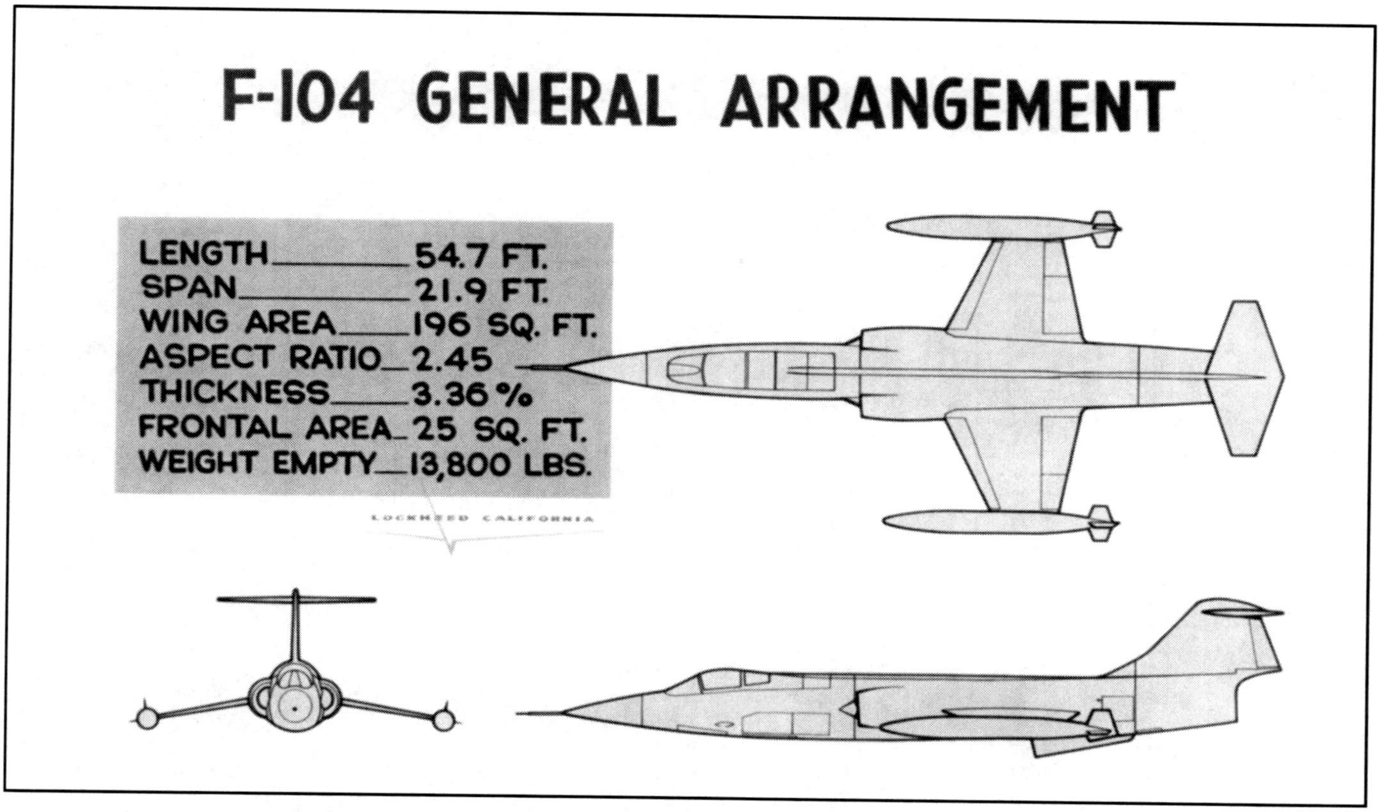

F-104 general arrangement, three-view and specs. (Lockheed Martin)

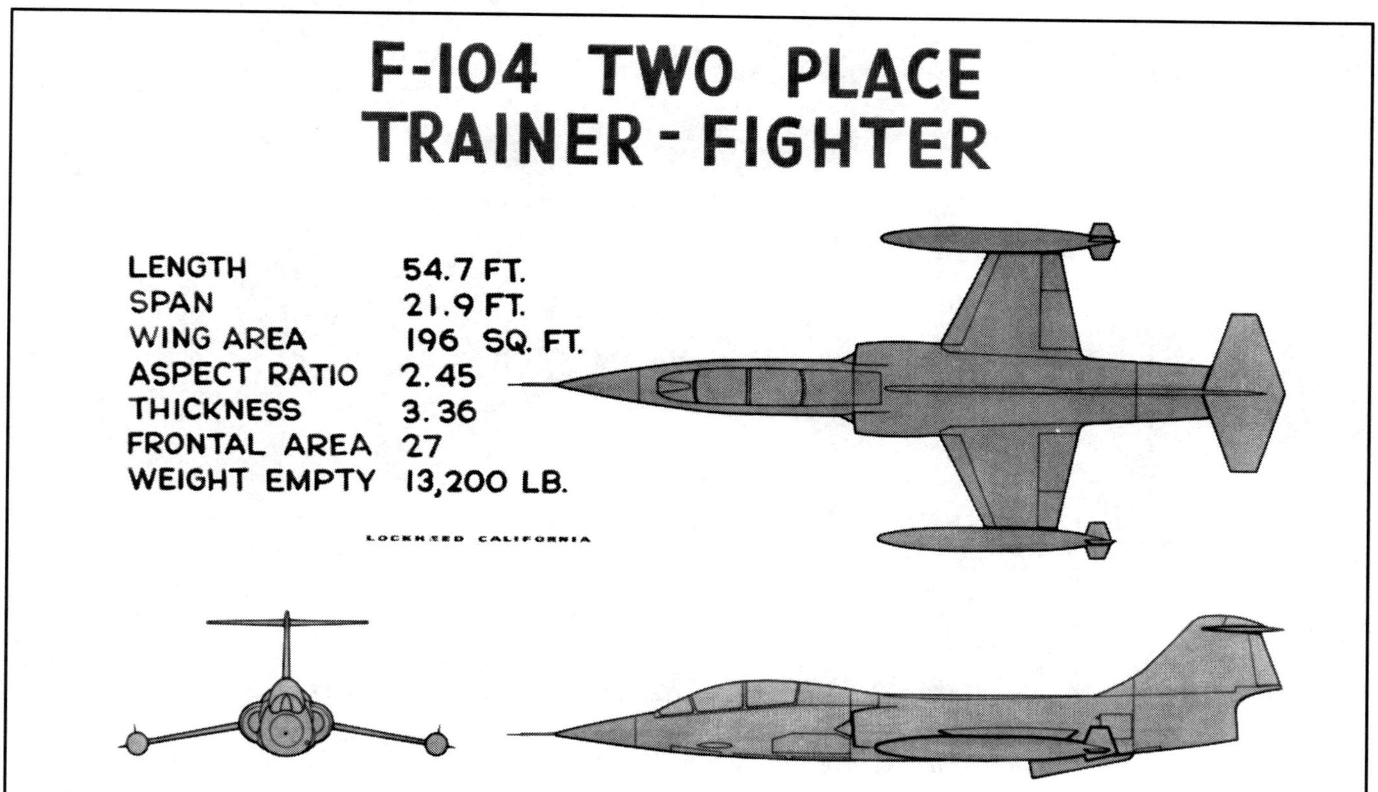

Two-place F-104 general arrangement, three-view and specs. (Lockheed Martin)

Aerial view of the Lockheed Palmdale final assembly production plant in the mid- to late 1950's. The two long buildings in the upper left are the production line buildings. The flight test facility is the large building at an angle in the upper center. Several types of aircraft in addition to the F-104s can be seen on the ramp in front of the flight test hangar. This was a very busy time at Lockheed. (Lockheed Martin via Tony Landis)

wiring and plumbing, was installed inside of these fuselage halves before they were joined together. Because of this modular assembly, the production time and costs were substantially minimized.

Only the fuselage mid-section and cockpit sections were manufactured at Burbank in Lockheed's main plant. All other components were made in other areas of the United States and Canada. The components were shipped to Palmdale, California for final assembly and flight-testing.

F-104 Production Numbers

Two XF-104 prototypes were originally built by Lockheed, followed by an order for 17 YF-104A service test and six production standard F-104As. Subsequently the United States Air Force ordered 147 F-104As, for the Tactical Air Command and the Aerospace Defense Command with another 26 two-seat F-104Bs, 77 single-seat F-104Cs, and 21 two-place F-104Ds.

Production of the F-104 took place at Lockheed plants in California and internationally. Lockheed-California facilities manufactured single and two-place aircraft for the USAF including those for the Military Assistance Program (MAP) and for the West German Air Force from 1956 to 1966.

Lockheed-California facilities manufactured "knockdown" assemblies for licensee use from 1961 to 1967. These were typically shipped to the licensee country's plant for assembly as the initial batch of the country's production run.

Worldwide manufacture of single-place aircraft was by Germany, Belgium, the Netherlands, Italy, Canada, and Japan. Co-production manufacture of two-place aircraft by Lockheed-California facilities

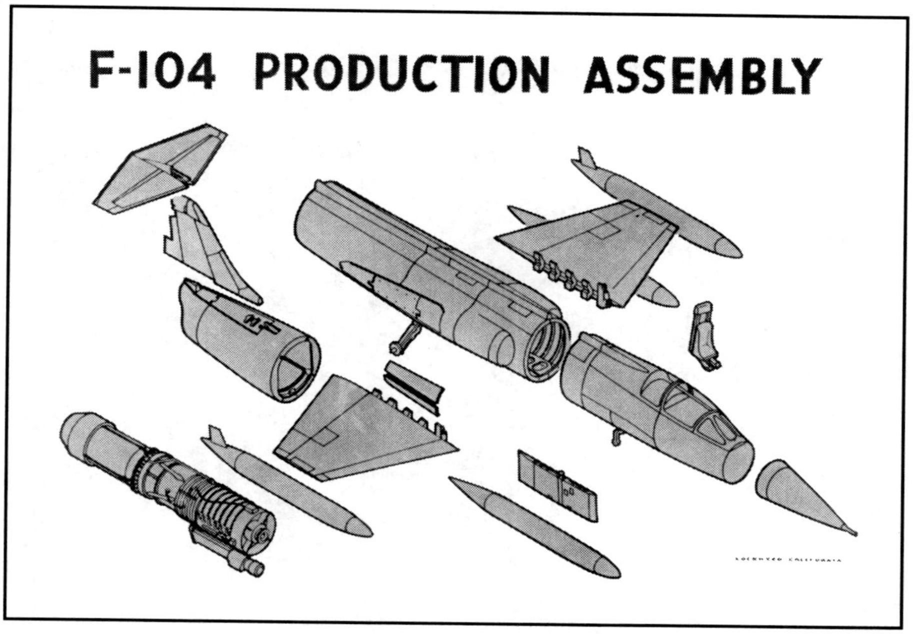

The F-104 was designed for production rates of up to 20 airplanes per day from a single assembly line. Breakdown of the major Starfighter components are shown. (Lockheed Martin)

Lockheed F-104 production line at Palmdale. (Lockheed Martin)

Lockheed production line for the F-104. (Lockheed, Jim Upton collection)

Lockheed Chief Engineering Test Pilot Herman "Fish" Salmon, wearing a partial pressure suit, stands by the nose of the YF-104A with metal covers over the inlets. The F-104 project was so secret that no photos were released to the public until April 1956, even though the XF-104 Starfighter first flew on 4 March 1954. Even at the April 1956 first public showing of the first production model YF-104A, the new engine inlets were covered by metal covers for security reasons along with the armament features being hidden, including the Vulcan 20-mm cannon. (Lockheed, Chuck Schisler collection)

and licensees Germany, Belgium, the Netherlands, and Italy were between 1964 and 1968.

NATO countries picked the F-104 as the fighter to meet their defense needs for the 1960s and 1970s, after an intense competition between Lockheed and several other aircraft manufacturers. A grand total of 2,578 F-104 Starfighters were built. Lockheed built 434 single-seat and 307 two-seat F-104s. 1,243 single-seat and 48 two-seat aircraft were built by NATO's European consortium, and 340 single-seat being built by Canada and 207 single-seat aircraft being built by Japan.

PERFORMANCE

Production F-104 Starfighters could climb to 40,000 feet in a minute and 40 seconds. This intercept capability along with its Mach 2 speed and ability to maneuver at Mach 2 while carrying Sidewinders made the Starfighter a formidable protector. The original 104's interceptor purpose would later change to a fighter-bomber role, in which it also performed very well.

F-104 FEATURES

PERFORMANCE, ENGINE, INLETS, AND SYSTEMS

The Lockheed F-104 Starfighter has many features unique to this double supersonic fighter. A look at the features and systems of the F-104 will give some insight into this distinctive aircraft. The F-104G, the model with the largest production run, is used in this description of features.

The F-104G is a single-place, lightweight, high-performance fighter-bomber powered by a General Electric J79-GE-11A turbojet engine with afterburner. Many combinations of air-to-air and air-to-ground weapons are carried by the F-104G for its various combat missions. The Starfighter has an extremely thin, high-speed wing, mounted well back on the fuselage with a 10-degree negative angle of dihedral. The 104 is also distinguished by its high horizontal stabilizer mounted on the top of the vertical fin.

Flight control system of the Starfighter is hydraulically powered, is irreversible, and includes stability augmentation about all three axes. Stick forces or control system "feel" are artificially developed by centering springs and a bob-weight. Two completely independent hydraulic systems are used, with either able to operate the control surfaces as a safety factor if one system is lost.

Electrically operated leading and trailing edge wing flaps with a boundary layer control system give the F-104 excellent low-speed handling qualities. Other features include: electrically operated 20-mm rapid-firing cannon; multipurpose fire control system; inertial and dead reckoning navigation systems; high/low altitude pilot escape system; main landing gear tires that permit operation from pierced plank and macadam runways; maneuvering-type autopilot; anti-skid brake system; and a variable-frequency, alternating current, electric power system.

SHAPE

Starfighter fuselage length is about two-and-one-half times as great as the wingspan. Wings are located far back on the fuselage and centered on the horizontal reference plane. The nose is "drooped" and the aft fuselage is elevated some from the horizontal reference plane. In flight the aircraft assumes a slight nose-up attitude, which corresponds to the minimum drag angle of attack. To accommodate this flight attitude, the pitot boom, air inlet scoops and engine thrust line are canted slightly with respect to the longitudinal centerline of the fuselage.

The aircraft's center of gravity range is interesting. It can vary from more than 20 inches aft of the wing leading edge at a lightly loaded landing weight to six inches forward of the wing leading edge at heavy take-off weights.

WING

How does the Starfighter fly on such a small wing? Data from supersonic rocket tests showed that the

The 24th production F-104A USAF s/n 56-736 in flight over Arizona. Negative dihedral of the thin short wings and high T-tail distinguish the F-104 from other "Century Series" fighters. The fuselage is two-and-a-half times longer than the wingspan. (Lockheed Martin)

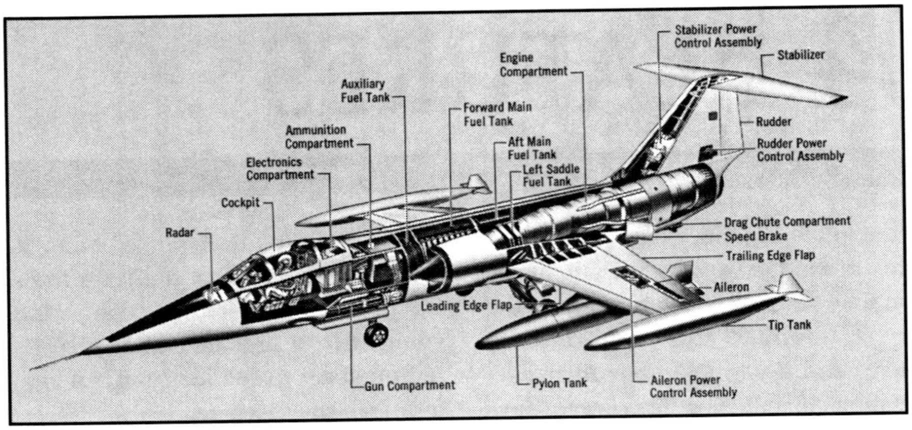

The Lockheed F-104 Starfighter is distinguished by its small size and extremely thin aerodynamic surfaces, as well as by its high horizontal stabilizer. The wing is mounted well back on the fuselage at a 10-degree negative dihedral angle. (Lockheed via Tom Laughlin)

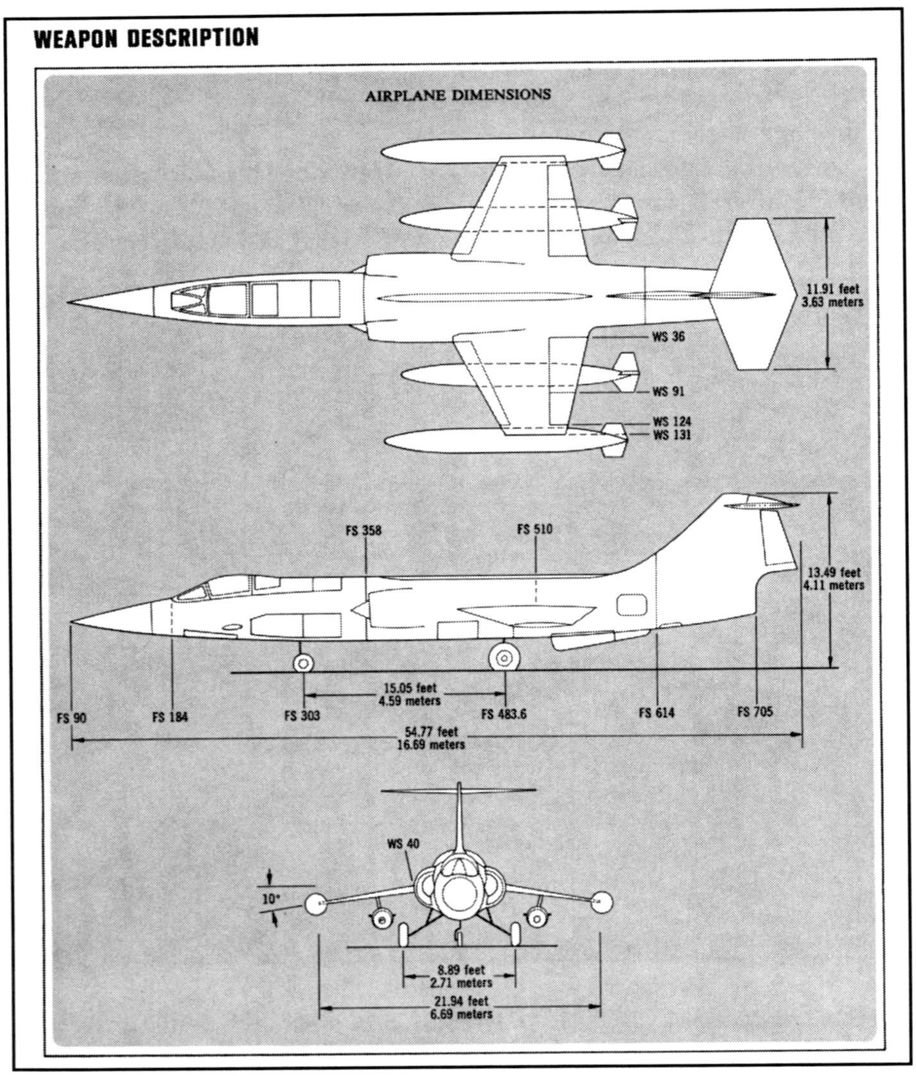

Three-view of the Lockheed F-104 with dimensions. (Lockheed via Tom Laughlin)

short straight wing had the better aerodynamic features for supersonic flight. Swept-back wings required a thick chord and a long span, with the resulting high drag to give comparable performance to the short straight wing. Also, extreme sweep resulted in deteriorated handling characteristics. The short wing reduces drag, and the effective wing area includes the amount of wing buried in the fuselage, so the wing is more effective than it appears.

Boundary Layer Control

To improve low-speed performance of the short wing, designers added wing leading edge and trailing edge flaps. These flaps convert the thin airfoil into a cambered high lift airfoil for take-off and landing. A Boundary Layer Control (BLC) system was also added to the Starfighter. To delay flow separation at full flap travel and to increase lift, the BLC system uses high-pressure bleed air blowing over the trailing edge flaps through orifices along the flap hinge line. The high-velocity boundary layer air greatly reduces the pressure just adjacent to the flaps and carries along the outer level of air, causing it to bend through the flap deflection angle. Results are a much slower landing speed.

Performance

The Starfighter has substantially more engine thrust than aerodynamic drag. The margin of extra thrust gives the F-104 its high speed and altitude capabilities, its high rate-of-climb, and its ability to carry fuel and weapons stores externally. Ability to maneuver at sustained supersonic speeds and ability to zoom to extreme altitudes well beyond its service ceiling are also possible because of the craft's excess thrust.

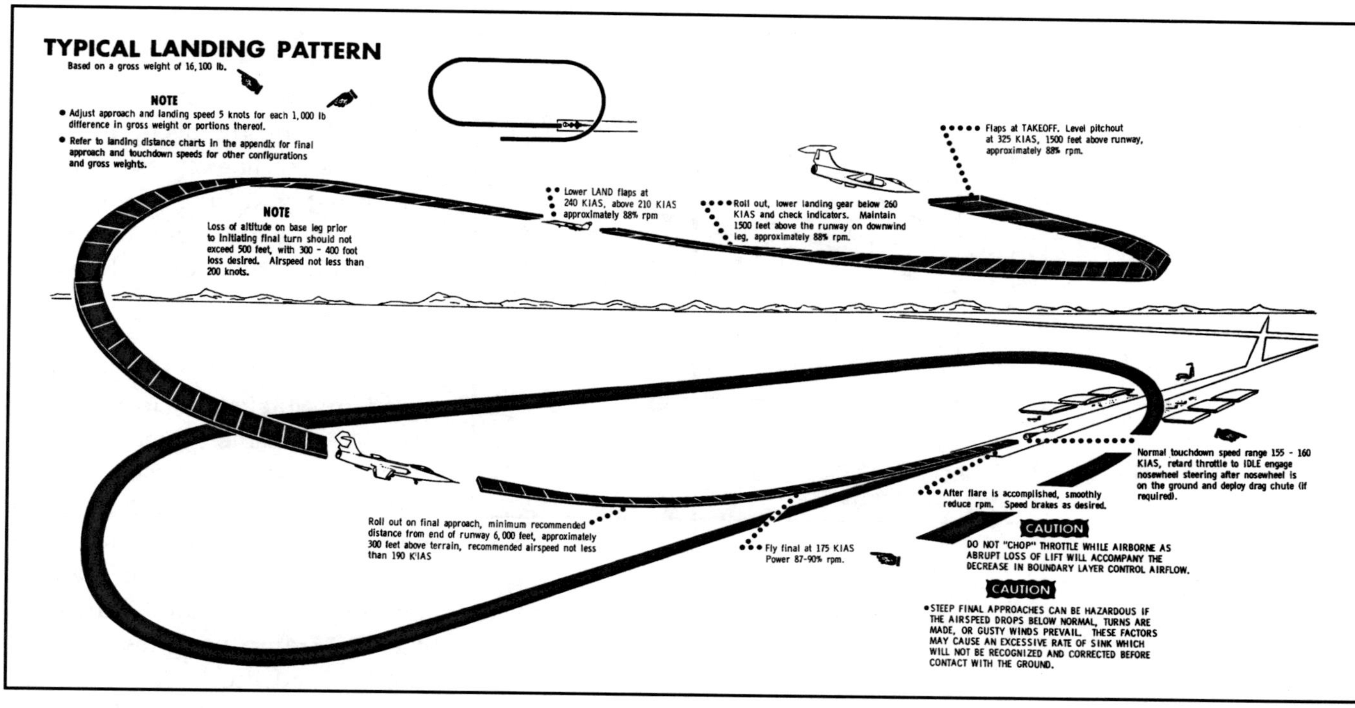

Standard landing pattern for the F-104G is performed with engine at 88% rpm starting at 325 knots 1500 feet above the runway, slowing to 240 knots with land flaps down on downwind, rollout on final with airspeed no less than 190 knots and touchdown at 155 to 160 knots. (John Whittenbury collection)

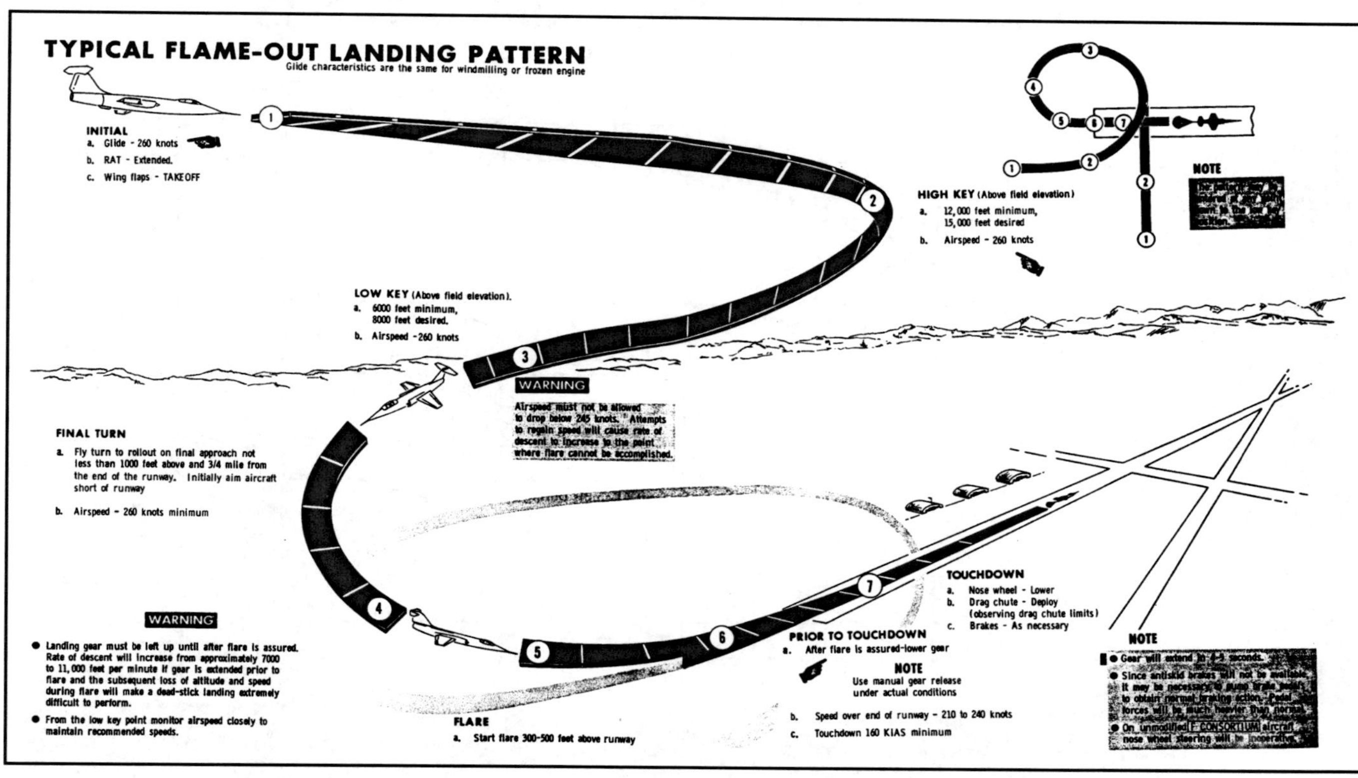

The flameout landing pattern is completely different from the standard pattern. A high key approach starts at 15,000 feet above the runway at 260 knots, and this speed is maintained through low key at 8000 feet and final turn at no less than 1000 feet. Speed over the runway is 240 knots and touchdown is no less than 160 knots. (John Whittenbury collection)

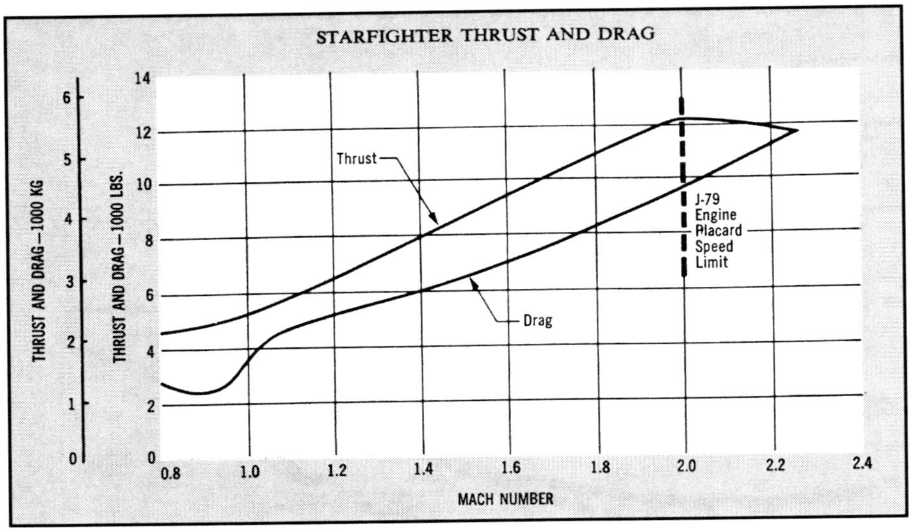

Thrust margin diagram shows why the F-104 is capable of continually accelerating even above Mach 2.0 if it were not for an engine temperature limit. (Lockheed via Tom Laughlin)

The F-104's margin of extra thrust provides a power reserve for acceleration, high rates of climb, and combat maneuvering at Mach 2.0. It also allows the F-104 to carry external stores and fuel at supersonic speeds.

Thrust Margin

Margin of extra thrust is shown graphically on the accompanying curve. The top line represents available thrust as a function of Mach number; the bottom line represents aerodynamic drag over the same speed range.

The curves show that drag is not equal to available thrust until a speed of Mach 2.26 is reached. Actually, available thrust is limited by the geometry of the inlet scoop and duct arrangement; therefore it could be extended to even higher Mach numbers except for the heat limitations of aluminum structure. Mach 2.26 approximates the sustained-speed limit for aluminum structure and is beyond the J79 engine temperature limits. The F-104 is "placarded" to a maximum

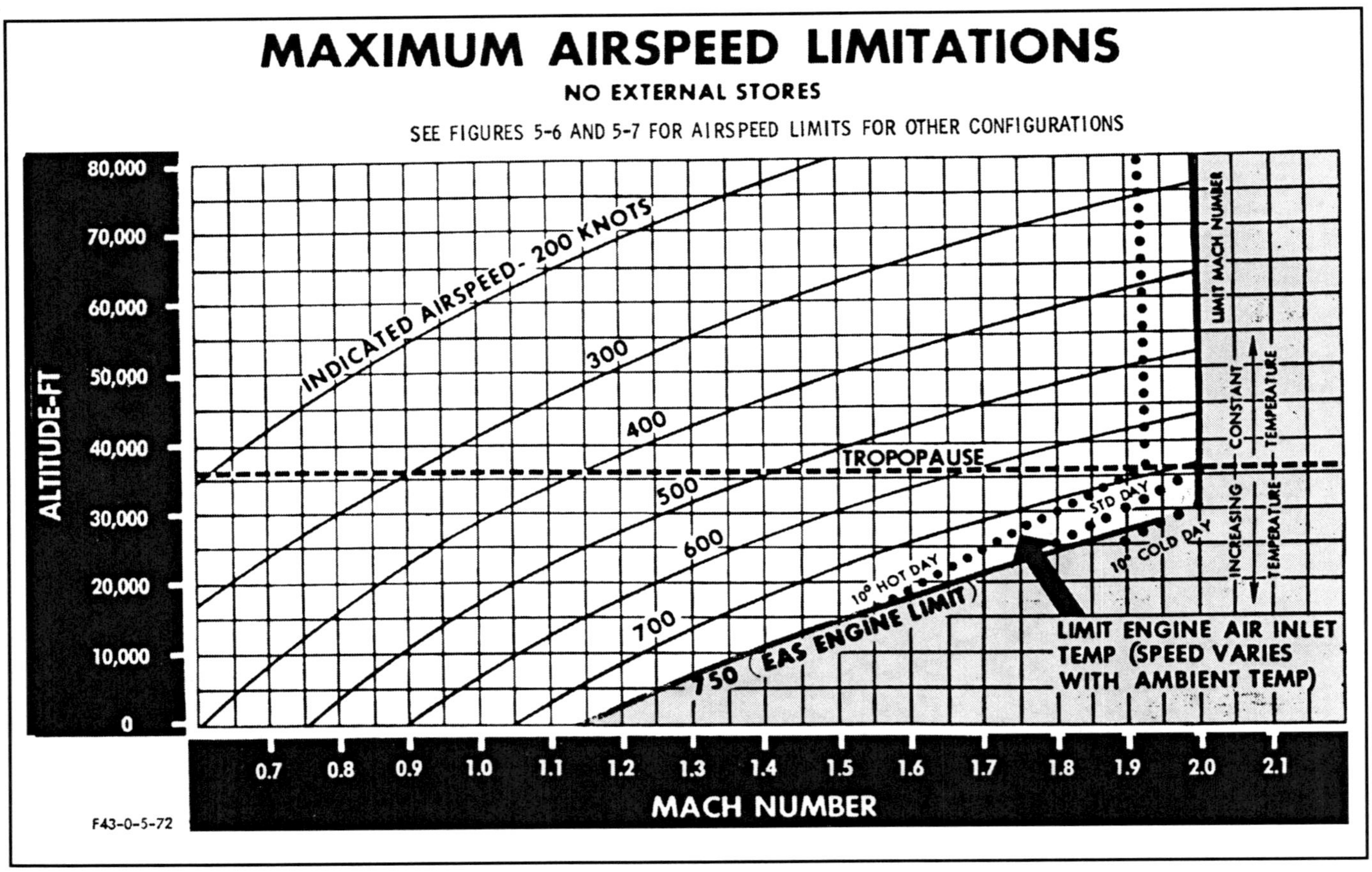

Maximum Mach and airspeed limits for the Starfighter are shown for various altitudes. (Lockheed via Tom Laughlin)

speed of Mach 2.0 because of these engine temperature limitations.

With maximum power at altitudes between 35,000 feet and the service ceiling, there is thrust available for climb, maneuvering, or emergency acceleration beyond Mach 2.0.

With military power (maximum power without afterburner), an aerodynamically clean Starfighter can sustain a slightly supersonic speed without using afterburner.

Climb Rate

If any single performance requirement could be termed the prime mover in the Starfighter's development, that requirement would be "superior climb characteristics." The F-104A Starfighter with Sidewinders and fuel for its mission can climb to intercept altitudes at a maximum climb rate of 60,000 feet per minute.

Carrying Sidewinders, the F-104 can climb and maneuver at Mach 2 without losing speed. The F-104 has enough thrust to carry it well beyond Mach 2 into a flight regime restricted by aerodynamic heating.

Zoom Maneuver

Altitudes well above the Starfighter's ceiling were attained by the zoom technique. This involved acceleration to speed at an optimum altitude, followed by a pull-up and climb at about a 45° angle. The maximum altitude attained was a function of speed at pull-up because higher altitude was attained at the expense of speed in a zoom maneuver. By exceeding the placard limit, the Starfighter has attained altitudes in excess of 100,000 feet.

A typical zoom maneuver commences at an altitude of 35,000 feet, a speed of Mach 2.00 and a load factor of 1.0. A Starfighter in steady-state Mach 2.0 flight at 35,000 feet represents kinetic energy equal to about 14,000 thrust horsepower, and this energy can be converted to additional altitude. Approximately 45,000 feet of altitude can be added. During the pull-up, load factor and altitude increase while speed decreases. As altitude is attained along the ballistic trajectory, load factor falls rapidly after the initial pull-up. As the Starfighter goes over the top, an altitude of over 80,000 feet is attained, Mach number is slightly above 0.4, and load factor is approaching zero Gs. During descent, speed and load factor build up as the initial altitude is approached.

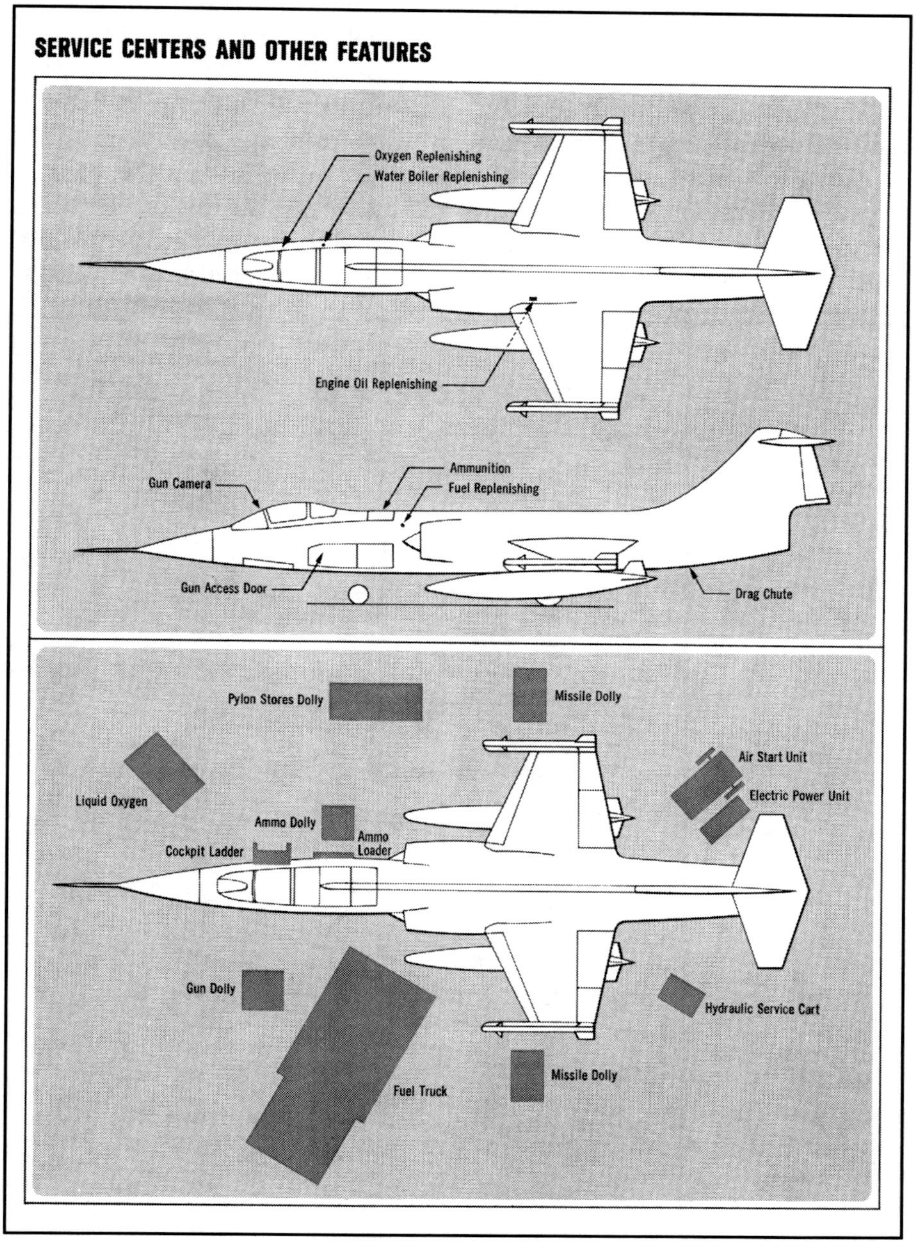

Servicing points are spaced around the Starfighter so that servicing operations can be conducted simultaneously without interference between personnel or equipment. (Lockheed, via Tom Laughlin)

Acceleration

The Starfighter's extra margin of thrust makes it possible to accelerate from subsonic to supersonic speeds in minimum time. This capability is essential for fast interception of supersonic enemy aircraft. For air superiority and combat patrol missions, the ability to accelerate quickly from cruise speed to intercept speed extends the Starfighter's mission duration without compromising its combat capability. The longer the time an interceptor requires to accelerate to combat speed, the higher — and therefore less economical — cruise speed it must maintain in order to enter combat with optimum effectiveness. The Starfighter can accelerate from its best subsonic climb speed to its placard speed of Mach 2.0 in less than three minutes at 35,000 feet altitude.

Time-To-Intercept

The Starfighter's combination of climb and acceleration capability was demonstrated on 10 December 1958, when the F-104 established a U. S. Air Force time-to-intercept record. Two Starfighters in combat trim intercepted a drone target, 150 nautical miles from their base, 8 minutes and 59.9 seconds after brake release. Target was between 35,000 and 40,000 feet altitude. The F-104 is well-suited for this type of mission, involving high climb rate, rapid acceleration, high speed, and maneuvering for closure and kill at high altitude.

The ability to accelerate in combat, whether it is for closing to attack, to intercept an intruder quickly, or to evade an attacker, is an indispensable requirement for an air superiority fighter. The F-104 can accelerate from subsonic speeds to Mach 2 in less than three minutes.

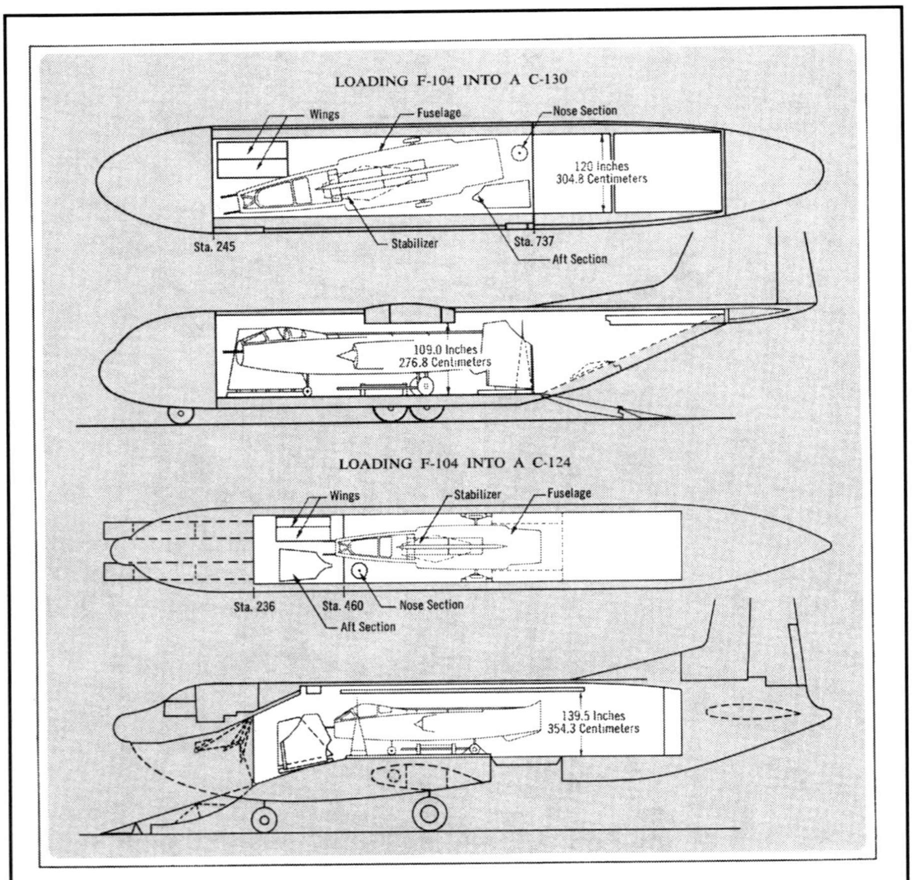

F-104 Starfighters could be air transported with minimum disassembly. A Douglas C-124 Globemaster or a Lockheed C-130 Hercules was capable of carrying a complete Starfighter. Empty weight of an F-104G was about 14,300 pounds. (Lockheed, via Tom Laughlin)

Maneuvering

Air-to-air combat superiority requires more than just rapidly attained level-flight speed. The speed that can be maintained while maneuvering for attack, or while evading an attacker, is a fighter's true useful speed. The F-104 has the thrust margin required to maneuver at supersonic speeds without losing air speed.

Extending the leading edge and trailing edge flaps gives the Starfighter good subsonic maneuvering ability for ground attack or for air-to-air combat at lower altitudes. Extending the flaps provides additional lift, which allows the F-104 to turn in a much shorter radius at subsonic speeds.

Emergency Overspeed Capability

The F-104'structure allows for emergency operation at Mach 2.2 in level flight (1 G load factor) at altitudes of 35,000 feet and above. Windshield panels and canopy are inspected following each such overspeed where the engine inlet temperature exceeds 250°F.

One J79 engine was operated at speeds between Mach 2.0 and 2.4 for 15 successive flights with no difficulty. In this speed range, the Starfighter was subjected to several 3.5 G pull-ups. These flights were conducted during the preparation and the successful attempt for the world altitude record in 1959.

The Starfighter can be landed at its maximum gross weight at somewhat reduced sink speeds. With no restrictive landing weight, it is not necessary to jettison weapons or fuel tanks before landing with high gross weights.

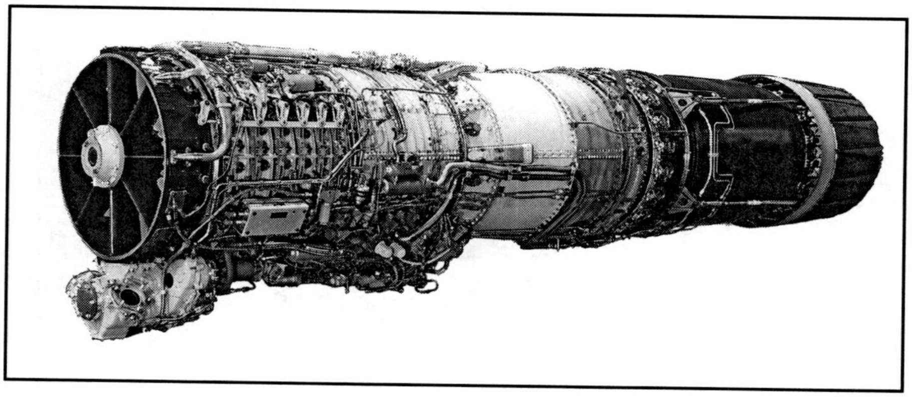

General Electric J79 engine. The J79-GE-7 engine produces 15,800 pounds of thrust. (General Electric)

General Electric J79

The Starfighter's J79 engine with afterburner is rated at 15,800 pounds of static thrust at sea level, weighs about 3,500 pounds, and is 208 inches long. The engine's 12-to-1 compression ratio assures high supersonic thrust, coupled with good subsonic fuel economy.

A J79-GE-11A axial-flow turbojet engine with afterburner powers the Lockheed F-104G. Major components of the engine are a 17-stage compressor section, an accessory drive section, a combustion section, a three-stage turbine, a high-thrust afterburner, and a variable-area exhaust nozzle.

At first glance it is a conventional turbo jet engine with a high compression ratio. Cool air entering the engine goes through the compressor section. Air is combined with fuel and ignited in burner cans. High-energy combustion products go through the exhaust turbine, which in turn drives the compressor blades. Afterburner section is located in the aft section. A feature of this engine is variable stators on the first section of the compressor. Also, the exhaust nozzle is continuously variable throughout the operating range of the engine. At idle speeds the nozzle is full open, at cruise power the nozzle reduces to its smallest cross section. In the afterburner range it gradually opens. The nozzle is fully modulated in the afterburner range.

These features permit the engine to operate somewhat like a ramjet, so that as the aircraft's speed increases the power being developed by the engine also increases at approximately the same rate.

Inlet

The air inlet arrangement is of primary importance to the power plant installation. The F-104 uses a fixed-geometry inlet scoop and a conical ramp arrangement, designed to give the best ram effect at speeds above Mach 1.5. The conical ramp projects ahead of the inlet scoop, creating a shock wave pattern at supersonic speeds. The shock wave slows the inlet air to a lower supersonic Mach number, while increasing the ram pressure at the inlet opening. The normal shock wave within the duct reduces the flow to a subsonic Mach number at high ram pressure.

One of the characteristics of supersonic flight is that, as speed increases, the inlet airflow volume increases more rapidly than do the engine's air requirements. Some Mach 2.0 aircraft have complex variable-geometry inlet systems to adjust

Night engine run on YF-104 55-2965 (msn 1011) at Edwards Air Force Base in May 1957. The flame from the afterburner is a spectacular sight at night. Heavy tie downs are required for these full-power checkout runs. (AFFTC)

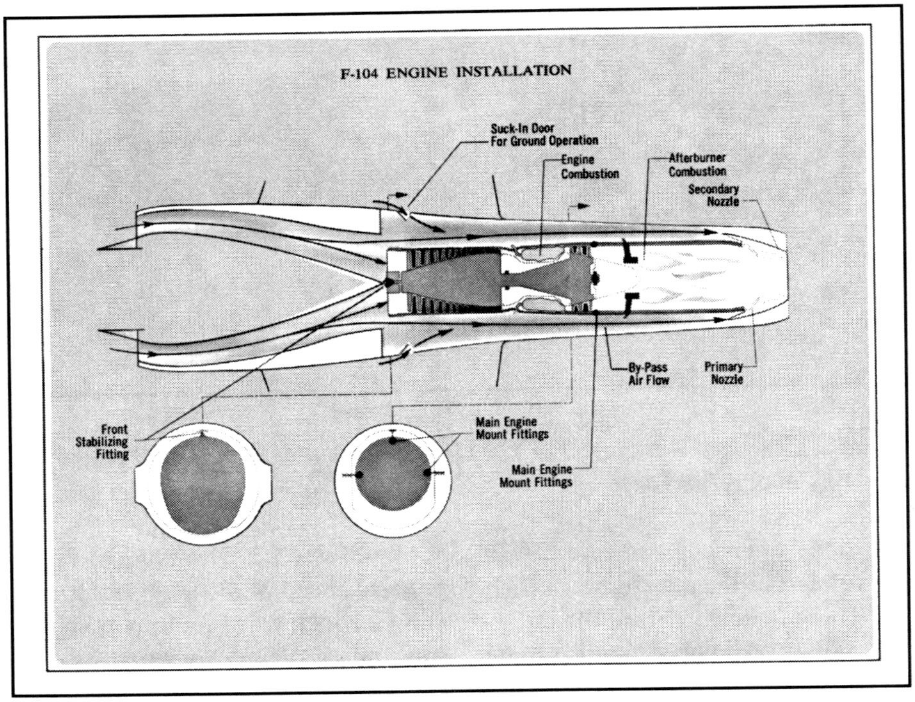

Engine and inlet diagram shows the airflow from the inlet to the engine face, and from the secondary airflow opening around the engine, exiting at the secondary nozzle. (Lockheed via Tom Laughlin)

Left side inlet on the F-104. The fixed cone slows the airflow down to subsonic speed before reaching the J79 engine, while the F-104 is flying at supersonic speeds up to Mach 2.2, over twice the speed of sound. The curved opening at back of the cone bleeds off excess airflow and ducts it through the engine compartment. The F-104 was the first aircraft to use a fixed inlet for slowing airflow to subsonic speeds to the engine. Most aircraft today use more complicated movable ramps and cones to provide the required subsonic flow to the engine. (Lockheed, Dave Steinbacher collection)

the airflow. Since the Starfighter's inlet area provides adequate flow for subsonic flight, it is oversized for speeds approaching Mach 2. The excess air would spill out of the duct and increase drag were it not for the F-104's secondary air flow system, which passes this air around the engine and out through the secondary exit nozzle. By-passing the excess air around the engine at high supersonic speed makes a variable-geometry inlet system unnecessary and obviates the maintenance and reliability problems inherent in such complex arrangements.

The F-104's principal deviation from conventional turbojet engine installation is the use of this secondary airflow to cool the engine and to improve the exit nozzle efficiency. (This function of the secondary airflow is described on the accompanying engine installation drawing.)

At supersonic speeds, excessive quantities of air enter the inlet duct, but this excess air is directed around the engine by entering the secondary airflow opening at the engine inlet. This arrangement allows the air to pass through the engine compartment with minimum drag and be ejected past the secondary exit nozzle in a manner that improves exit nozzle efficiency.

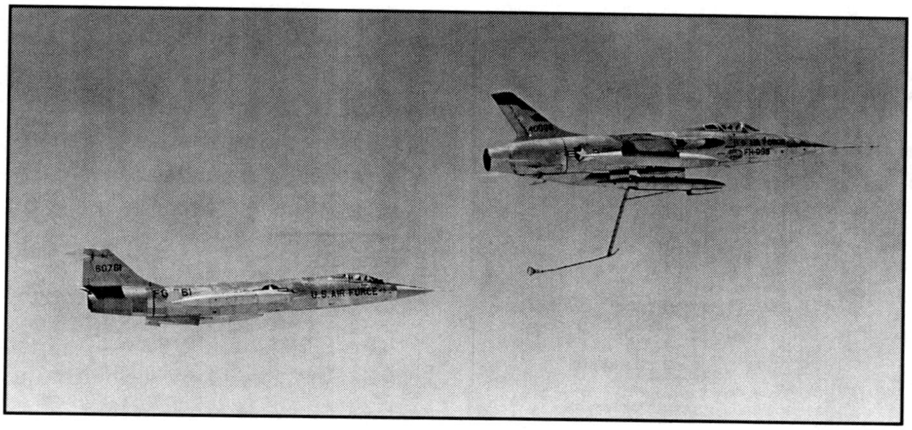

Republic YF-105A refueling F-104A msn 1049 on June 24, 1958. Jet speeds are better matched by another jet. This was a test of the fighter-to-fighter in-flight refueling system at Edwards Air Force Base. (AFFTC History Office via Tony Landis)

When the engine is running on the ground, a low-pressure condition exists at the front face of the engine and at the throat of the secondary exit nozzle. To avoid a reverse flow of air around the engine, spring-loaded suck-in doors are installed in the fuselage exterior so that air can be drawn into the engine compartment. The flow of air entering through the suck-in doors divides, with some moving forward to the front of the engine and some moving aft to exit through the secondary exit nozzle. The airflow aft serves to cool the entire engine installation.

Engine Flow

Engine turbine is the three-stage impact type and is connected directly to the compressor. Gases impinge on the turbine buckets, causing the turbine wheel to rotate. This in turn drives the compressor, sustaining the flow of air through the engine.

In the afterburner section, fuel is sprayed into the discharge of gases from the turbine. Oxygen, still present in the discharged gases, supports combustion of the afterburner fuel, which results in a large thrust increase. The throttle lever controls supply of fuel to the afterburner section. Several increments of afterburner thrust augmentation are available between zero and maximum.

Exhaust ejector has a variable nozzle which automatically adjusts the area of its opening as required. Nozzle functions as a variable restriction through which exhaust gases are accelerated to their maximum velocity for maximum thrust. The nozzle also controls pressure and temperature in the tailpipe by selecting the optimum exhaust area for greatest thrust, at any power setting, from idle through afterburner range.

Fuel System

The F-104 fuel system provides five bladder-type fuel cells installed in the fuselage. The fuel cells have a usable fuel capacity of 896 U. S. gallons, and this amount is considered the basic aircraft capacity. Depending on mission requirements, as much as 852 gallons of additional fuel can be carried as follows: two wing tip tanks, 340 gallons; two wing pylon tanks, 390 gallons; three optional fuselage tanks, 122 gallons. Optional fuselage tanks are constructed of metal and replace the M-61 gun, its ammunition container, and the expended case storage container.

Starfighter's wing-tip and pylon fuel tanks provide a combined additional fuel capacity of 730 gallons. Use of external tanks was established in the initial design as a means of extending ferry range, combat radius, and patrol time duration. External tanks that can be jettisoned allow extra fuel to be carried without compromising the F-104's air-to-air combat configuration. Carrying all fuel internally would have required a larger airframe, which would impose weight and drag penalties.

External tanks are easily installed or removed and can be jettisoned in flight. Fuel is transferred from the external tanks to the main tanks by means of bleed air pressure from the engine compressor. This is a convenient means of using the externally carried fuel first and maintaining maximum quantity in the fuselage tanks as long as possible.

The Starfighter's tanks can be refueled, either individually through conventional gravity-flow fillers, or from a single-point filler when pressure-fueling facilities are available.

F-104 has provisions for installation of an aerial refueling probe. The probe connects to the single-point fueling adapter and projects up along the left side of the cockpit. This gives the pilot a good view of the probe during its engagement with the tanker drogue. Both internal and external tanks can be filled in flight. The probe is easily installed and removed, and when installed is used for both ground and air refueling.

Bleed Air System

Bleed air systems are those systems that depend on discharge air from the engine compressor for their operation. Three high-pressure air bleed ports at the engine compressor's 17th stage are provided for this

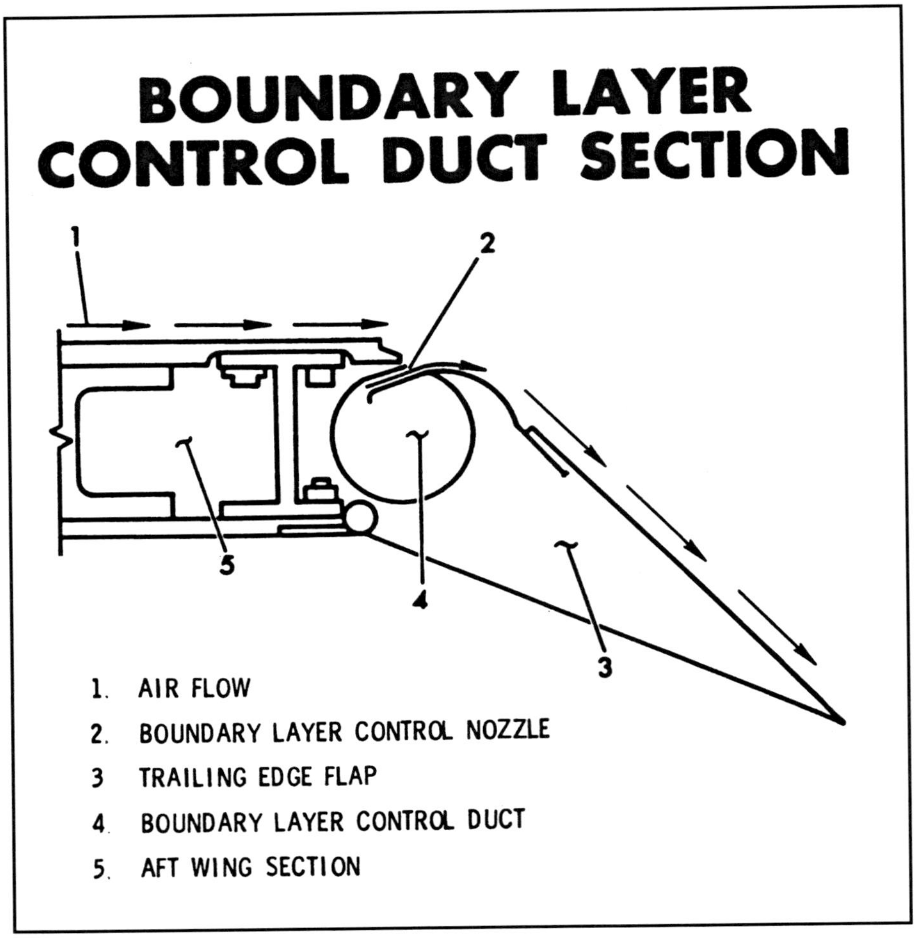

The Boundary Layer Control (BLC) system gets its air from the last compressor stage of the engine. The BLC manifold has a series of nozzles that direct this high-pressure high-temperature air over the upper surface of the flap when the "LAND FLAP" position is selected by the pilot. (John Whittenbury collection)

purpose. A port on the right side supplies air to the boundary layer control duct at the right trailing edge flap. A similar port on the left side supplies the left duct, both for Boundary Layer Control. A port at the top left side of the engine supplies air to all the other systems.

The fuel transfer system uses bleed air pressure for its operation. Air pressure forces fuel from the external tanks into the fuselage aft main fuel cell. Fuselage fuel cells also are maintained at positive pressure in order to prevent their collapse when a rapid change of altitude causes a sudden change of atmospheric pressure.

The air conditioning and pressurization system also uses engine bleed air. A refrigeration unit in the system supplies properly conditioned air to the cockpit and electronic compartment. This ensures the pilot's comfort, cools the electronic equipment, and also pressurizes the cockpit and electronic compartment.

Other uses of bleed air are: the hot air jet rain removal system, which keeps the left windshield panel free of rain; pressurization of the canopy and electronic compartment hatch seals; cooling and pressurization of the radar nose package; windshield and canopy defogging and defrosting; gun gas purging; and providing pressure for the pilot's anti-G suit. Bleed air is also used for defogging and defrosting the viewing windows for the internally mounted reconnaissance camera system.

Hydraulic System

The F-104 has two completely independent, closed-center hydraulic systems for normal operation. Each of these systems is served by its own engine-driven, constant-pressure, and piston-type hydraulic pump. If either of these systems should fail, the other will maintain operation of the flight controls at a reduced rate. There is also an emergency hydraulic pump, which is driven by a ram air turbine that can be extended into the air stream to supply hydraulic power for reduced-rate emergency operation of the primary flight controls.

Flight Controls

The Starfighter's primary flight control surfaces and speed brakes are hydraulically actuated. Its wing flaps and trim system are operated electrically. The F-104's primary flight control system consists of hydraulically powered rudder, ailerons, and a one-piece horizontal stabilizer. The secondary flight control system incorporates leading and trailing edge wing flaps for increasing lift and speed brakes for increasing drag. A further increase in lift for landing is achieved with the boundary layer control system which blows bleed air, from the 17th engine compressor stage, back over the trailing edge flaps, when they are extended to the landing position.

Primary flight control surfaces are actuated by servos that are powered by the number 1 and 2 hydraulic systems. Input signals are sent to the servos from the pilot's control stick and rudder pedals, from the stability augmentation system, and from the trim and autopilot systems.

Stability Augmentation

Stability augmentation system provides maximum stability of the F-104 in any flight attitude or maneuver. Rate-sensing gyros detect any sudden change of attitude about the aircraft's three axes and produce electrical signals proportional to the deviation they have detected. These signals, after being amplified, are sent to the proper control surface servo valve, which then produces the proportional surface adjustment to correct the attitude. A synchronous transmitter on the servo valve supplies a feedback signal that cancels the original signal, causing any oscillation to be damped.

Trim system is powered and controlled electrically, and the trim actuator output is connected mechanically to its respective servo valve input arm.

Flaps And Brakes

Wing leading and trailing edge flaps are positioned by electromechanical actuators. A flexible shaft interconnects the drive motors for each wing to synchronize the flaps and to enable one motor to drive both flaps should the other malfunction. The two speed brakes are hydraulically powered and electrically controlled. They operate in synchronization and the pilot may select any position between "full open" and "full close."

Autopilot

The autopilot system controls attitude in roll and pitch through its aileron and horizontal stabilizer actuators. The system provides heading hold in conjunction with either altitude hold or Mach number hold. The pilot can use the control stick steering provisions to maneuver the airplane in autopilot without disengaging the system. At any time the pilot can override the automatic control.

The automatic pitch control system functions as a stall-prevention device. Inputs from an angle-of-attack vane and a pitch rate gyro are fed into a computer which, when the aircraft first approaches a stall, causes the pilot's control stick to shake as a warning. Should the nose-up attitude be continued until a stall becomes imminent, the computer commands a pitch signal to a hydraulic servo,

Italian F-104S on landing approach with the speed brakes out. (MAP)

F-104 speed brakes, left and right, are electrically controlled and can be adjusted by the pilot to any position between full open and full close. (Lockheed, Dave Steinbacher collection)

Close-up view of the landing gear on a German F-104G. The circular shaped landing light is mounted on the upper door. Main wheel well door is just cracked open in this photo. (Jim Upton collection)

which quickly and firmly moves the control stick forward while also positioning the horizontal stabilizer for a nose-down attitude. Visual indication of the pitch attitude is presented to the pilot on the instrument panel. Like all automatic functions of the flight control system, the automatic pitch control can be overridden by the pilot.

Landing Gear

While the Starfighter's wings were not thick enough to house its main landing gear, wheels and tires, a gear was developed which retracts into the fuselage. The F-104 is equipped with a tricycle-type retractable landing gear. All three units of the gear retract forward into the fuselage by hydraulic power. In the event of hydraulic failure, the gear can be released manually and will fall into the "down and locked" position for landing.

A device called a "liquid spring" supports each main gear strut. This unit provides shock-absorbing action through a special fluid that compresses under load. A special filler permits adjustment of the fluid pressure for the F-104's various operating weights. Main wheels have hydraulically powered anti-skid brakes. The steerable nose wheel is mounted on a conventional shock-absorbing oleo strut.

Landing Drag Chute

Use of the Starfighter's landing drag chute shortens landing distances by 10 to 20 percent. The longer the landing distance, the greater the percentage of that distance can be saved by deploying the chute. The reason for the difference in effectiveness is that total ground roll increases with increasing touchdown speed, and the drag induced by the chute increases as the square of the speed. Therefore the drag chute is more effective at high touchdown speeds.

The chute is the conical ring slot type, and has a diameter of 18 feet. It is stowed at its point of attachment in the lower aft section of the fuselage. The pilot deploys the chute with a pull-handle in the cockpit. After the aircraft has slowed, the pilot can release the deployed chute from the aircraft.

Arresting Gear

An emergency arrester hook is installed so that it can engage an overrun cable at the end of the runway. The hook is not for use on an aircraft carrier, as some observers have wondered, but is an emergency-use item adequate for stopping a heavily loaded F-104, even at high ground speeds. An arrester hook is installed in the aft lower section of the fuselage. An electrically

Landing gear retraction during take-off of a Canadian CF-104. The landing gear retracts forward and rotates into the fuselage. The emergency arresting hook can be seen on the aft bottom of the fuselage. The hook is used for engaging an overrun cable at the end of a runway. (Lockheed, Dave Steinbacher collection)

Drag chute deployed for shortening landing distance on the F-104. Here, the deployment is part of the Svetkoff's Starfighters Inc. air show routine at Jacksonville Naval Air Station in 1998. Two Starfighters land at the end of their routine, one uses the drag chute and the other uses aerodynamic braking, holding the nose off the ground as long as possible, creating more drag to slow the aircraft. (Pete Clukey)

operated actuator/damper cylinder similar to a shock-strut cylinder extends the hook. When extended, the hook engages an arresting cable on the runway for emergency stops.

The hook is designed to engage a cable up to one inch in diameter, which is limited to a maximum restraining load of 60,000 pounds by the cable loading system. The F-104 arrester hook installation was qualified for both "water-squeeze" and chain-drag cable-loading systems.

The Starfighter may also be arrested with an MA-lA runway barrier. Hooks to engage the barrier are installed at the forward edge of the main gear doors. An F-104 with tip tanks can be arrested with an MA-lA barrier at any speed between 40 and 120 knots. Centerline and pylon stores are jettisoned before engaging the barrier.

Cockpit

Flight instruments are grouped together on the upper panel with the engine instruments located on the right-hand area. Armament controls are also grouped together. Radar

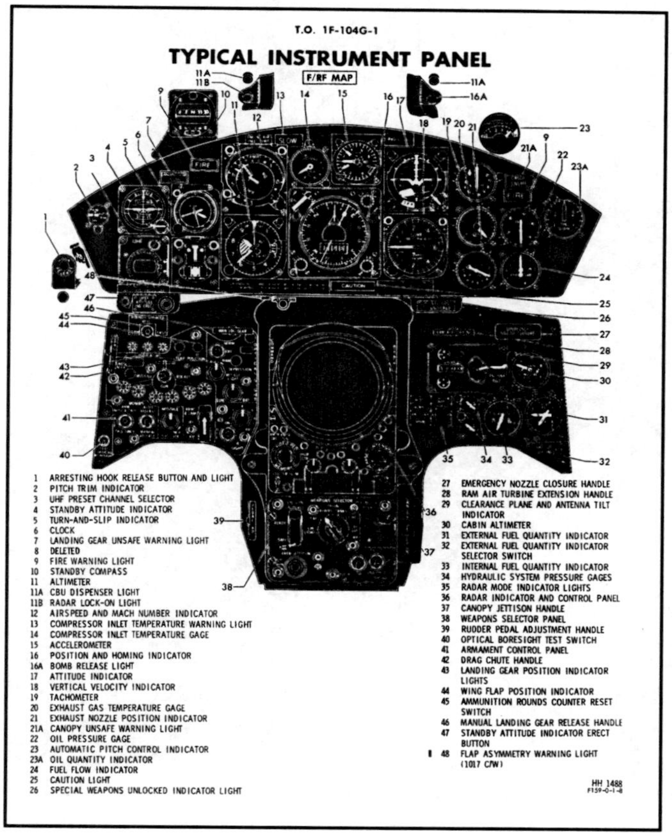

Details of the F-104G cockpit instrument panel. (John Whittenbury collection)

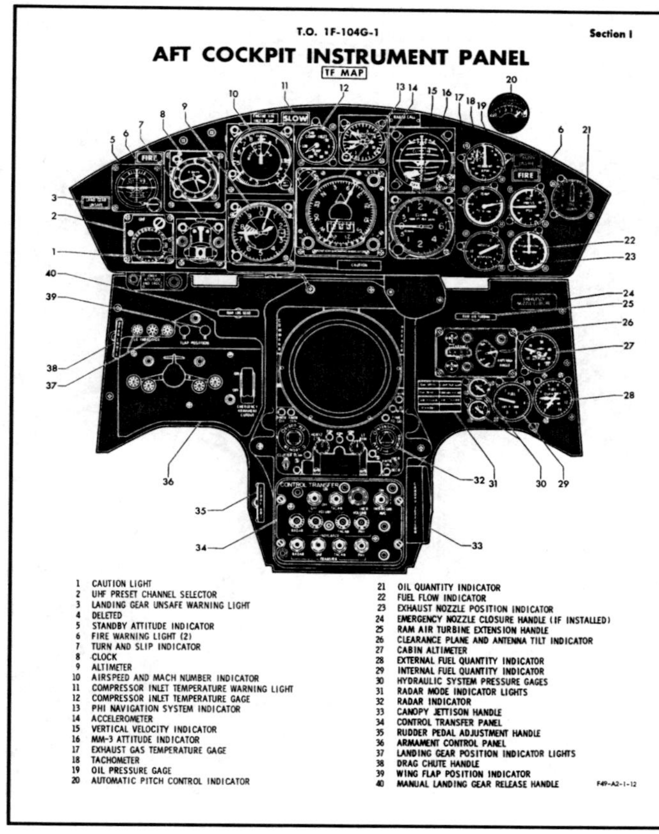

Details of the TF-104G aft cockpit instrument panel. (John Whittenbury collection)

scope and controls are located on the lower instrument panel directly in front of the pilot.

An important feature of the basic cockpit design is the elimination of multiple warning lights. There is one master caution light located in the center of the main panel together with a multi-panel of annunciator strips, each indicating a function. In the event of difficulty, the master caution light goes on together with the system indicating the trouble. The pilot noting the condition can reach up and push the master warning light out, while the annunciator panel light remains on. This warning system is also used on the Lockheed T-2V Sea Star, L-188 Electra and Jet Star.

The F-104 features two fire warning lights and also something new in aircraft: the "Slow" warning light. It was provided to warn the pilot that he had reached a thermal barrier (a limit on the engine temperature). A temperature probe measures air temperature entering the engine and sets the slow light to flashing "Slow" "Slow" "Slow," when the critical temperature is reached.

Control panels for various systems are mounted on the side consoles. Panels are of uniform width, and all are mounted in a similar manner. Several panel locations are wired so that optional fire control, navigation, and reconnaissance system controls can be quickly substituted.

Instruments

The instrument panel in the F-104 cockpit was designed for the best possible readability and accessibility. The upper panel contains flight and engine instruments; the radar scope and centerline bomb controls are centered below. On the pilot's left are instruments and controls related to landing gear, flaps,

Cockpit of the F-104. Flight instruments on the upper left and center panel with engine instruments on the upper right panel. Radar and armament control panels are on the center console, and oxygen and communication controls are on the right side panel. (Lockheed, Dave Steinbacher collection)

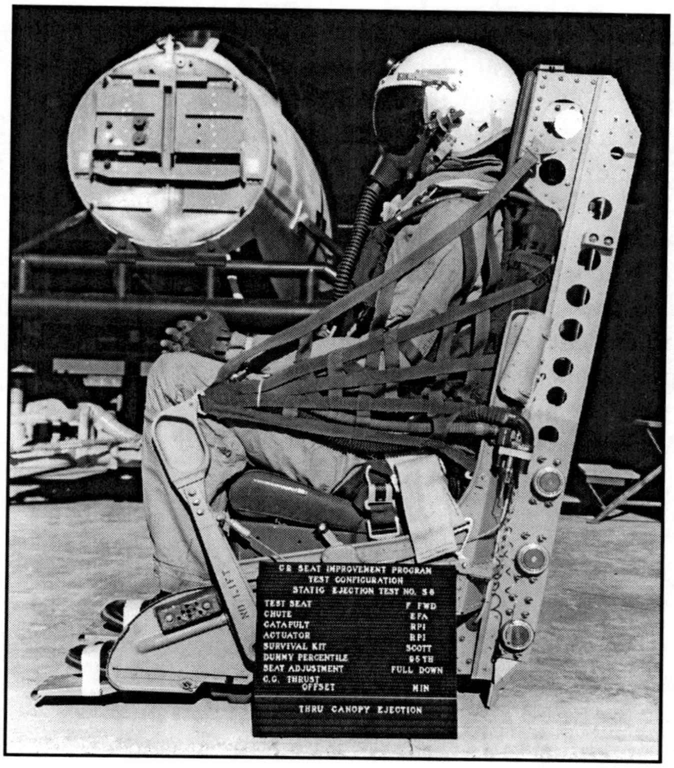

Left: *The C2 upward ejection seat replaced the earlier downward ejection seat for the F-104. A dummy was used for the sled tests of the ejection seat.* (Lockheed, Dave Steinbacher collection)

Right: *Full pressure suits, similar to the astronauts' suits, were used for high-altitude flights in the F-104. Standard F-104s could reach 90,000 feet in zoom maneuvers, and this altitude required a full pressure suit. In this photo the pilot is climbing into an NF-104, which had a 6,000-pound thrust rocket in the tail and could reach altitudes over 120,000 feet. Notice the four reaction control nozzles in the lower right part of the photo.* (Lockheed, Dave Steinbacher collection)

and armament; to the right are instruments and controls affecting the radar mode, fuel load, and cockpit environment. There is also a series of system warning lights. All instruments are illuminated for night flying, as are the printed placards affecting aircraft operation.

Escape System

The F-104 is equipped with an emergency escape system consisting of a canopy that can be jettisoned and an upward ejection seat. The rocket catapult ejection seat provides escape at ground level, if an air speed of at least 90 knots indicated has been attained. Maximum speed for ejection is approximately 550 knots EAS (Equivalent Air Speed). Canopy jettison is included in the normal ejection sequence, or the canopy may be jettisoned separately.

The seat incorporates an automatic system for separating the pilot from the seat at its trajectory peak. The seat has an oxygen supply for high altitude bail-out and a survival kit that is carried with the pilot at bail-out.

Rocket cylinder for the seat is mounted to give the seat forward as well as upward thrust. Resulting trajectory provides clearance over the high T-tail on the 104, should the pilot have to eject at high speed.

For high altitude ejections, the chute deployment is delayed until the pilot descends to a lower altitude at which time a barometric pressure-sensing element causes the chute to deploy. During the pilot's descent, oxygen for breathing and for inflation of the pressure suit is supplied from the emergency oxygen cylinders in the survival kit.

During flight at low altitudes, the pilot connects a zero-time-delay lanyard that deploys the chute immediately following the separation sequence. The Starfighter's zero-altitude ejection seat system permits safe escape for the pilot at forward speeds as low as 90 knots. This is below the Starfighter's sea-level stall speed.

Avionics

When the F-104G evolved from earlier versions of the Starfighter, the principal area of new design and development was in its light-weight, integrated, multipurpose electronic system. The electronic system comprises approximately 7% of the Starfighter's weight when empty and represents approximately one-third of its material cost.

Major electronic systems include communication and identification system, navigation and basic flight reference, Automatic Flight Control System (AFCS), and the fire control system. Most of the Starfighter's electronic equipment is located in a compartment just aft of the cockpit. Systems are individually packaged in special containers developed so that an entire F-104 system can be quickly checked out or replaced.

Jeep Cans

A "Jeep can" on the F-104 is a packaged box or unit containing various electronic items. Each was shaped to fit precisely into the electronics compartment. They all had the same shape with the same height and depth but could vary in width.

Individual "Jeep Cans" were on a shock-mounted rack with electrical connectors and central cooling air distribution hook-ups. Each set contains a built-in test circuit, permitting personnel to quickly determine if equipment was operating correctly during preflight. If it was not, rotating the top handle and lifting it out quickly replaced the complete package. These packages were referred to as "Jeep cans" because of their similarity in size and shape to the gasoline containers carried on the military Jeeps.

Inertial Navigator

The F-104's inertial navigator system provides the precision navigation information required for all-weather strike/bombing missions. It serves as the primary vertical reference for attitude information and is the principal directional reference for heading information. Its outputs are supplied to the PHI, attitude indicator, and bombing and fire control systems. Inertial navigator is a completely self-contained system that functions without receiving or emitting any electro-magnetic signals that could be detected or jammed by an enemy. The inertial navigator supplies position, heading, bearing, and/or attitude signals to the PHI, attitude indicator, autopilot, and fire control systems.

For flights requiring accurate navigation, sufficient time must be allowed for system warm-up and fine alignment (usually 10-15 minutes, depending upon ambient temperature). However, for alert intercept missions, the system can provide the necessary attitude and heading information in as little as 60 seconds.

PHI System

The Position and Homing Indicator (PHI) system continuously computes and displays navigation information. It accepts data from several sources within the aircraft and then translates it into range and bearing information displayed on the PHI instrument. The system operates in three navigation modes: inertial, dead reckoning and TACAN.

The obvious advantage of the PHI system is that the pilot is not burdened with time-consuming and tedious navigation chores that would detract from performance of the combat mission. The PHI continuously displays the aircraft's magnetic heading, as well as the grid heading, station bearing and range to any of 12 selected points within a 1,000 nautical mile radius, providing the distance between aircraft and station is less than 1,000 nautical miles. The station selector can be pre-set with geographic position coordinates of up to 12 in-route checkpoints, destinations, targets, alternate bases, etc

Many of the systems used in the Lockheed F-104 had to be designed specifically for the Starfighter, as there were no other aircraft flying at the speeds and altitude at which the F-104 flew.

Tops of avionics "Jeep cans" can be seen near the top of the ladder of this Belgian F-104G. This avionics packages were called "Jeep cans" because their size and shape were similar to the WWII gas cans. They provided quick change and check-out of the avionics systems. (MAP)

3 FLIGHT TEST

ADVANCED CHALLENGES

The Lockheed F-104 was the subject of the most extensive flight test program ever undertaken by any fighter aircraft of its time. The program was comprised of three main categories: the ground and lab test programs which were prior to flight testing; the Lockheed flight test program; and the Air Force flight test program.

The total span for these test programs, if laid end to end, amounts to 600 months or about 50 years. Obviously many of the programs were carried out simultaneously. The flight test programs themselves involved approximately 10,000 flights, and over 60 test aircraft were used in the program.

The Lockheed F-104 Starfighter was more thoroughly shaken down than any other combat aircraft to date before entering service. Test locations were spread out at USAF base locations including Eglin AFB Florida, Ellison AFB Alaska, Edwards AFB California, Holloman AFB, New Mexico, Hamilton AFB California, Wright-Patterson AFB Ohio, and at the Lockheed production facility at Plant 42 in Palmdale, California.

XF-104 TESTING

The first XF-104, USAF serial number (s/n) 53-7786, was trucked to Edwards AFB North Base in late January 1954. First flight occurred on 4 March 1954 with Lockheed test pilot Tony LeVier at the controls. Testing progressed rapidly between January and the arrival of the second XF-104 nearly a year later.

The second XF-104, USAF s/n 53-7787, was the first equipped with the considerably more powerful afterburning Wright J65-W-7 engine. This engine was also retrofitted to s/n 786, replacing the non-afterburning Wright J65-W-6. Lockheed test pilot Ray Goudey achieved a speed of Mach 1.79 (1,324 mph) on 25 March 1955 flying s/n 787. This was the highest speed attained by either of the two prototype XF-104s.

On 18 April 1955, Lockheed's Herman "Fish" Salmon was flying

Number 1 XF-104 on the dry lakebed at Edwards Air Force Base. The XF-104 initially had a non-afterburning Wright J65 engine. "786" was trucked to Edwards AFB North Base in late January 1954. First flight occurred on March 4, 1954 with Lockheed test pilot Tony LeVier at the controls. Notice the location of the National insignia on the aft fuselage. (Lockheed, Dave Steinbacher collection)

The second XF-104 USAF S/N 53-7787 was the first to have the considerably more powerful afterburning Wright J65-W-7 engine. Lockheed test pilot Ray Goudey achieved a speed of Mach 1.79 (1,324 mph) on 25 March 1955, flying s/n 787. This was the highest speed attained by either of the two prototype XF-104s. (Lockheed, Dave Steinbacher collection)

787 on a gun-firing test when an explosive decompression occurred. Misdiagnosed as a Gatling gun failure, Salmon ejected successfully using the downward ejection seat. Tony LeVier had run into gun difficulties earlier in the same aircraft. Investigation revealed that the explosive decompression was caused by the loss of the bottom ejection seat hatch fairing.

Prototype flight-testing continued with the other XF-104 s/n 786, with the USAF accepting the aircraft in November 1955. The XF-104 flight-testing eventually spanned three years. First flight of the XF-104 was on 4 March 1954. Two hundred fifty hours were accumulated on the Wright J65 powered XF-104 before the first flight of the General Electric J79 powered YF-104A on 17 February 1956. The YF-104A reached Mach 2 on 27 April 1956.

The YF-104A and subsequent models were five feet six inches longer than the XF-104 in order to accommodate the larger GE J79 engine. YF-104s were initially flown with the General Electric XJ79-GE-3 turbojet engine, which had 9,300 pounds thrust dry and 14,800 pounds in afterburner. The XJ79-GE-3 engine was later replaced with the J79-GE-3A with an improved afterburner. Other changes to the YF-104As compared to the XF-104s included a forward retracting nose gear, modified inlets with half cone center-bodies, and two additional fuel cells in the fuselage.

Flight testing activities included 35 F-104A production models in addition to the 17 YF-104As. Progressive changes were made during the flight test program, including airframe strengthening, the addition of a ventral fin to improve directional stability at supersonic speed and the addition of Boundary Layer Control (BLC), a flap blowing system. The BLC improved landing characteristics with a slower landing speed.

F-104 Recollections

A sense of what went on during flight test of a new aircraft in the 1950s and '60s can be gained from the brief stories of some of the flight testers who were there.

Stalls And Pitch Up, A Very Wild Ride!

Dick Fetty, a Lockheed F-104 Flight Test Analysis Engineer, recalls a wild early characteristic of the F-104. "Test Pilot Tony Levier experi-

Preflight taxi run on the number one XF-104 in February 1954 at Edwards Air Force Base. Notice the extended speed brakes. The XF-104 was a classified program and no photos were released until April 1956. (Lockheed, Dave Steinbacher collection)

enced the first stall and pitch-up. He was so impressed that he landed immediately and retired to the debrief room at Pancho Barnes place.

"Early in the F-104 program, the Aerodynamics Engineers had gone to the USAF proposing that an automatic pitch control be installed, but the Air Force was not interested. Tony's experience was the convincer.

"During the early stall tests, the airplane was modified to allow venting of fuel from the wing tips to allow a chase airplane to photograph a pitch-up. These films were dramatic and showed the airplane when it got about 15 degrees angle of attack how it would rapidly pitch to about 60 degrees up and oscillate laterally and directionally and then suddenly yaw and roll out of control.

"The A.O. (Automatic Observer, a camera photographing a duplicate instrument panel of the cockpit) and oscillograph records of these events were also quite dramatic. They clearly showed an airplane basically tumbling and descending at sink rates of 12,000 to 15,000 ft/min.!!

"Pitch up occurred in all flap configurations of the airplane and only at aft CG (Center of Gravity) would it enter into a spin.

"During the development we had four or five airplanes flying these types of tests, and I would get data reduced and provide the preliminary data analysis so that Bill East and Joe Carrillo could plan the day's testing. If my memory serves me correctly, a total of about 2500 test flights were flown to finalize the system, and there were significant development problems. This system had to automatically protect against pitch-up in any type of maneuver from a 1 'G' to an accelerated 'G' entry. We started out with a simple angle of attack vane sensor on the forward fuselage that was set to operate the stick shaker and pusher

Both prototype XF-104s in formation flight in early 1955 near Edwards Air Force Base. This photo was taken from a North American B-45 Tornado that was used as an engine flying test bed. The wing-tip fuel tanks on "786" did not have any tank fins at this early stage. (Lockheed, Dave Steinbacher collection)

XF-104 "786" with horizontal fins on the tip tanks. Tip tank oscillations were investigated during flight testing and resulted in several tip-tank fin configurations with various tank sizes. (Lockheed, Dave Steinbacher collection)

Number 1 and number 2 XF -104s in flight over the Mojave Desert. Both XF-104s had the considerably more powerful afterburning Wright J65-W-7 engine after 786 was retrofitted, replacing the non-afterburning Wright J65-W-3. (Lockheed Martin via Tony Landis)

Ejection seat sled with dummy in the cockpit. In front of the dummy is a high-speed movie camera lens used to record the ejection as the sled goes down the test track. (Jim Upton collection)

(I called it what it was, a kicker; 60 pounds plus!) at an indicated angle of attack that was guessed at.

"We used a pitch rate gyro as the rate input but incorporated a washout of the signal to allow full capability of maneuvering. This was the solution.

"We now had a working and reliable system, but we had not demonstrated it throughout the flight envelope under all speed, altitude and entry conditions. The difficult area was to demonstrate safe protection for a maneuver entered as a straight maximum rate pull up at the corner of the V-G envelope where the airplane is limited at 7.33 g's. This maneuver required the pilot to pull full back stick and hold it until the kicker saved his butt. To my knowledge there were only two test pilots who had the confidence and patience to hold that stick full back until the kick pushed the nose down. Those two pilots were Ray Goudey and Ed Brown, two of the best Engineering Test Pilots in this business."

Dick Fetty

Ejection seat test. The rocket-powered sled is shot down the track and the ejection seat is fired at the target speed. High-speed cameras are in the sled and outside along the track to record the ejections. (Jim Upton collection)

Gun Problems

Art Troutman recalls a startling result of a problem with the Gatling gun during flight test.

"My perspective at the time was that of a tech writer, covering such subjects as armament, so I was not as directly involved as were those in flight test & the 104 design project. One phenomenon was the curiosity of the bird making a climbing left (or right?) turn upon trigger depression! It turned out to be a momentary sag in bus voltage, due to the tremendous current flow through the gun motor (a virtual short circuit). This voltage drop then manifested itself as an unintentional climbing L(R) turn "command" through the automatic flight control system.

"And there were a number of problems regarding 'gun gases'. Of course, we all remember that classic, horrid experience of Tony's. As I recall, the main fix was to purge the gun compartment with engine bleed air. Of course, in solving one problem, quite often one creates a new problem. As I understand it, at altitude, the J79 was always going to be susceptible to any reduction in intake air (or even a reduction in its oxygen content - as in purged gun gases entering engine intake ducting). A related problem then occurred regarding spent round cases and the related links. Retaining these hot rascals on board could fire off any unfired rounds (like riding on top of the ultimate popcorn machine) or igniting any residual gun gases. So let's eject these suckers - where they can get sucked into the engine intake scoops (the ultimate FOD!). So let's provide an ejection rail. But if that's out in the breeze - what a drag! So let's make it automatically extendable. Of course, 'dear old Lockheed' again was the first airframe manufacturer to utilize such a revolutionary concept an airborne Gatling gun. So we were stuck with 'getting stuck' with all the growing pains - the price of being at the cutting edge of new technology. I think of all the problems we ran up against in advancing the state of the art in such programs as the F-104, YC-130, U-2, A-12, YF-12, SR-71, F-117, and on and on, including those we still cannot discuss, and I had the privilege of being involved in all of them, as a tech writer and a design engineer. Getting back to the 104, we solved all of those problems, a tribute to everyone in flight test and the design project."

Art Troutman

Number two YF-104A, USAF s/n 55-2956, with the metal security covers installed over the inlets ready for the first public showing in April 1956. Even though this new combat aircraft with twice the speed of the previous operational aircraft had been flying for over two years, no public photos had been released. When performance of the F-104 was still classified, the inlets were covered because aerodynamicists could figure out the optimum speed of the 104 from the shape of the inlet cones. (AFFTC)

Number nine YF-104A, Air Force s/n 55-2963, at Elmendorf AFB, Alaska, for cold weather testing. This aircraft was assigned to the Air Force Flight Test Center at Edwards AFB, California, and was deployed to Elmendorf for the cold weather testing. (Lockheed, Dave Steinbacher collection)

F-104 Tip Tank Oscillations

Dave Gill, a Lockheed Flight Test Analysis Engineer on the F-104, recalls the flight test investigation of F-104 fuel tip tank oscillations.

"The oscillation was an up-and-down movement of the nose and tail of the tip tank at about 4 Hz (cycles per second). The tank motion was very noticeable to the pilot, as was the ride in the cockpit because tests showed side accelerations reached .3 to .4 g's. It generally occurred below 15,000 feet and around .8 Mach with half-empty tip tanks. This 'phenomena"' had occurred on an F-104B at EAFB and later on F-104G S/N 1089. I believe the pilot was a German fellow named Birkenbiel.

"The S/N 1089 oscillation was limit cycle (sustained) and lasted about five seconds, at which time the yaw damper was turned off. The oscillation immediately stopped. After the airplanes were in service, reports came in from the field of this 'phenomena' and a flight test program was conducted at Luke AFB in 1966.

"The aircraft was a Luke bird with a history of tip tank oscillations. It was instrumented for wing loads and had accelerometers in the tanks and cockpit. A wagger or oscillator was used to drive the rudder and/or ailerons through the dampers and was also found to produce larger tip tank oscillations than pilot-induced control pulses. Our tests were done with 800 pounds of fuel in each tank, as that was where wing loads were greatest. It was found that the yaw damper was extremely influential in sustaining or stopping oscillations. The roll damper was less of a factor, but an interesting thing was that the pilot's hand on the stick could (due to the cockpit lateral motion), increase the inertia of the system and result in an increase in the magnitude of the oscillation. This could be further exacerbated by rotating the forearm into the lateral motion; the pilot was essentially a servomechanism in a closed loop having the effect of increasing roll damper gain.

Number 10 YF-104A USAF s/n 55-2965 with no security covers over the inlets. Four external fuel tanks are installed. Seventeen YF-104A production prototypes were built for flight-testing the aircraft and systems. (AFFTC)

"We never could induce an oscillation, even with the wagger, when damper gains were properly set, even in moderate to heavy turbulence. We could, though, with high yaw damper gains and in fact did encounter a self-starting oscillation when passing over a mountain ridge in moderate turbulence. It stopped as soon as the gain was reduced to the proper setting.

"Wing loads never went above 50 % of design limit, and it was concluded the oscillation would not lead to structural failure. The yaw damper was the primary culprit and a failed feedback or malfunctioning feedback circuit could also play a role. Yaw damper potentiometer settings varied considerably among operational aircraft and could not be relied on as a direct indication of actual gain. Functional tests of the damper were recommended using a highly sophisticated device, a pencil attached to the control surface and a piece of cardboard to scribe surface movement on.

"As a result of the tests, a flight manual supplement was issued and to my knowledge we never had the problem again. There probably were more, but most likely correcting the yaw damper gain was the explanation and we never heard about it."

Dave Gill

Lockheed test pilot Ken Weir at the nose of the F-104S with number of "kills" (mission completed symbols) on the fuselage. Weir was responsible for shooting down four of the five drones shown. (See "Boola Boola" in this chapter.) (Lockheed via Jim Fitzgerald)

Technique For Testing Tip Tank Oscillations

Dick Fetty, a Lockheed F-104 Flight Test Analysis Engineer, recalls some flight test techniques.

"Dave's discussion reminded me of the problems we ran into during these tests. The analysis method (archaic today) wouldn't work when the Pilots input aileron control movements, and caused a lot test repeats. The pilot input was caused by the lateral forces while he was gripping the stick. I was constantly complaining to the pilots to not allow aileron inputs. This was very difficult for them during a lateral directional oscillation that could be of significant amplitude with very low damping. It was particularly difficult in a turn at elevated g's where the spiral mode would come in and try to roll the airplane. Test pilot Ed Brown had a unique method to keep ailerons centered. He would place both elbows on the cockpit sill with his forearms extended close to but not touching the stick throughout the oscillation. He would sometimes end up nearly inverted during the test. We usually asked the pilot to allow the oscillation to go for five or six cycles.

"Although our test method would be considered archaic today, we were able to define safe operating limitations for all external configurations that were approved for flight at high Mach where directional stability was of concern."

Dick Fetty

Boola Boola

Chuck Price, a Lockheed F-104 Flight Test Avionics Engineer, recalls some interesting testing of the weapons system on the F-104S.

"This recollection has to do with the F-104S flight test program conducted in Palmdale in the 1967-1970 time frame. Among other features of the 104S was the Raytheon fire control system for the AIM-7 Sparrow missile. The flight test program called for live firings of the AIM-7 against Ryan Firebee drones over the Pacific Missile Range. A telemetry system was installed in the test aircraft and a small receiving station was set up on the ramp in Palmdale in order to monitor the performance of the missile and the fire control

Left: *Two F-104Cs on take-off from Palmdale. In flight refueling, probes are installed on the left side of both aircraft.* (Lockheed, Dave Steinbacher collection)

Right: *Boeing KB-50J refueling a Lockheed YF-104A during the test program. The KB-50J version of the Boeing B-50 bomber had two 5,200 pound thrust GE J47 jet engines in addition to the four reciprocating engines. This increased the speed of the KB-50J to 444 mph at 17,000 feet altitude, better matching the faster jet receiver speeds. Speed difference between a prop and jet aircraft is significant.* (AFFTC)

system during these tests. On the day of the first live firing, things were tense, to say the least. The telemetry van was a crowded place. One of the parameters displayed on the brush recorders in the van was a Doppler closing signal with an accompanying audio signal relating to missile lock-on.

F-104G of the German Air Force in the climatic hangar at Cold Lake Canadian Forces Base, Canada in December 1961. A complete range of temperature conditions can be supplied under controlled conditions in the climatic hangar. All aircraft systems are operated at the extreme temperatures for reliability testing with temperatures from –65 degrees F to + 120 degrees F. The climatic hangar can also duplicate rain and humidity conditions found almost anywhere in the world. This type of testing usually lasts about two months. (Lockheed, Dave Steinbacher collection)

"The test pilot for this first live firing was Ken Weir. When Ken locked on to the drone and fired off the AIM-7, all the data displayed in the telemetry van were positive. After a period of time, the missile audio stopped chirping and the Doppler trace had marched across the brush recorder. One of the engineers in the van was a Raytheon field service rep. whose name escapes me. All of a sudden he yells 'Boola Boola'! We all looked at each other and asked, 'What's Boola Boola'? Well, in missile speak it signifies a direct hit with a near miss being just 'Boola'. Ken Weir had scored a direct hit on the drone with the first live shot of an AIM-7 from a F-104S. Needless to say, a lot of blood, sweat, and tears had led up to that first live firing mission. There were more 'Boola Boolas' and 'Boolas' to come. I think Ken was our ace by the end of the program, but Bill Weaver, Jack Woodman, and Art Peterson participated in the flying duties as well.

"There were other mods to the aircraft, including the -19 version of the J79, installation of electrically operated inlet doors, an additional hydro generator and other items I have forgotten. I believe this was one, if not the last F-104 flight test program, conducted at Palmdale. The L-1011 was on the horizon. We had a great team and it was a fun time."

Chuck Price

F-104 T-Tail Flutter

Dick Heppe, project aerodynamics engineer during the start of the F-104 program, recalls the problems and resolution with T-tail flutter.

"Without question, the single most difficult technical challenge encountered in the XF-104 and F-104A development programs was the catastrophic flutter problem of the unique T-tailed empennage configuration. Overpowering aerodynamic and mechanical design considerations drove the center of gravity of the horizontal tail mass well aft of both the bending and torsion axes of the vertical tail, upon which it was supported. This created a classical flutter machine unless the torsion and bending stiffness of the vertical surface was high enough to prevent occurrence.

"Though structural characteristics were straightforward and predictable, the transient aerodynamics of the configuration at transonic speeds and very high dynamic pressure were almost completely unknown. Thus the design envelope for the aircraft of Mach 1.2 at sea level created an extremely difficult and unpredictable situation. Both analysis and actual wind tunnel flutter model testing clearly demonstrated that the tail was highly vulnerable under the right conditions. All of this was proven conclusively when one of the XF-104s (msn 1001) lost its empennage in high speed, low altitude flight during flight test."

High-speed camera footage of the Lockheed F-104S firing AIM-7 Sparrow II air-to-air missiles during flight test. (Lockheed, Jim Fitzgerald collection)

Bill Park was flying the XF-104, chasing Bob Matye in the F-104A during a tail flutter test. The XF-104 had a lower limit Mach than the F-104A and apparently reached the flutter limit sooner than the F-104A. Park successfully ejected after the tail separated from the aircraft, using the downward ejection seat.

"The heart of the problem was our inability to define with any precision what the vertical tail bending and torsion stiffness requirement had to be for safety. Various assumptions on the transonic aerodynamics led to a wide range of differing stiffness requirements. But which was correct? There was no way to pin it down.

"At this time the production F-104A was rapidly coming together, and something had to be done. The solution that endures to this day is a fascinating example of seat-of-the-pants engineering in the face of monstrous unknowns. Lacking any specific definition of the stiffness requirements, engineering technical management worked with manufacturing to determine the maximum thickness of stainless steel box covers that could be installed utilizing the production tooling. The answer came out to be 1/4 of an inch. The decision was made to go to 1/4 inch, solid stainless steel box covers on the vertical tail. It worked!!"

"Every F-104 built around the world thereafter used the steel box covers. There was never a single case of aircraft loss to T-tail flutter in decades of operation. How about that for science?"

Dick Heppe

DC-3 Flying Test Bed

How do you test elaborate electronics in a single-place aircraft?

F-104 chase missions included chasing some exotic aircraft like the Lockheed Mach 3 M-21 carrying a D-21 drone. While the Mach 2 F-104 could not keep up with the M-21 for the whole flight, it still provided a valuable service as the external eyes for the M-21 crew, who could not see the drone from their cockpit. (Lockheed via Tony Landis)

Seven F-104s on the flight test ramp at Lockheed Palmdale. Included are Canadian, U.S. Air Force, and German F-104s. The DC-3 flying test-bed in the background has an F-104 nose and F-104 radar and avionics installed. (Lockheed, Dave Steinbacher collection)

Lockheed's engineers, faced with the task of providing an electronics package to do a big job but which could be packed into the limited space of the 104, and which would withstand extremes of temperature and vibration, enlisted the services of the company's old DC-3 as a test bed.

The aircraft was given a tapered "Pinocchio" type nose containing the s/n 1046 F-104 radome, while the fuselage was packed with a complex array of electronics gear, a cockpit mock-up, banks of test and measuring equipment, and room for a team of engineers to monitor the systems operation during flight.

The DC-3, with its eight-foot long beak, became a well-known sight as it carried out 50 flights during an intensive program lasting 16 weeks. Equipment tested on board included the radar optical sight, in-range computer, bombing computer, TACAN receiver, inertial navigator, air data computer, and the PHI dead reckoning navigator system. The "see-through" quality of a new plastic filament-wound radome for the 104 was also flight-checked.

50s Flight Testing

Flight test in the 1950s was a lot different than it is today. Slide rules and calculators were an engineer's primary tools, rather than the computers of today. When you look at the flight test challenges that were overcome on this very advanced aircraft of the 1950s, it is remarkable.

F-104 Models

XF-104 Through F-104S

A total of 16 major models of the Lockheed F-104 were built. Models were not only built by Lockheed in the United States, but also by companies in Europe, Japan, and Canada. Any given model could be built by more than one aircraft manufacturer. The table in Appendix 'B' includes a breakdown by model and manufacturer. The following is a summary of details and differences of the various F-104 models.

XF-104

Two XF-104s were built in the Skunk Works prototype shop. The prototype XF-104s were originally powered by non-afterburning Wright XJ65 engines producing 10,200 pounds of thrust. Later, J65-W-7 engines added an afterburner, which produced a higher thrust. XF-104s did not have the conical inlets. Empty weight was 11,500 pounds, and maximum speed with the Wright engine was Mach 1.79. Maximum range was 800 nautical miles. The XF-104 was 49.17 feet long — 5.6 feet shorter than later models. Wingspan remained the same on all F-104 models except the NF-104A. Armament on the XF included the M-61 Gatling gun, the type K-19 fire control system and the AN/APG-34 Radar.

YF-104A

Seventeen YF-104As were built as production prototypes. They had a lengthened fuselage to 54.77 feet and the higher-thrust J79-GE-3A engine, which produced 14,800 pounds of thrust in afterburner. The new supersonic conical inlets were first used for the YF-104As. All succeeding models had the GE engine and conical inlets.

F-104A

Lockheed built 153 of the first production model F-104A. The "A" models had the J79-GE-3A engine, which produced 14,800 pounds of thrust. Maximum speed was Mach 2.0 and range was 1,444 nautical miles with tip tanks and pylon tank (dropping the pylon tank when it was empty). Empty weight was 12,562 pounds and maximum takeoff gross weight was 24,528 pounds. The F-104A had five pylons, one on the fuselage and four on the wings.

Armament consisted of an improved M61-A1 Vulcan gun, two AIM-9B Sidewinder air-to-air missiles, with the AN/ASG-14T-1 fire control system. During operational service the downward ejection seats were replaced with the Lockheed designed C-2 upward ejection seats, and the ventral fin was added on the bottom of the fuselage and Boundary Layer Control (BLC) was added to the flaps.

XF-104 msn 1001 in flight. The XF-104 made its first flight on 4 March 1954. Only two XF models were built, and both had the Curtis Wright J65 engine, as the General Electric J79 was not available at the time. The XF-104 was shorter than later models by 5.6 feet. Wingspans were the same on all F-104s except for the three NF-104As. (Lockheed, Dave Steinbacher collection)

Production model F-104A carrying Sidewinder missiles. Notice the ventral fin on the bottom of the fuselage. A fuel line runs through the spine on top of the fuselage. During operational service the downward ejection seats were replaced with the Lockheed-designed C-2 upward ejection seats and Boundary Layer Control (BLC) was added to the flaps. (Lockheed, Dave Steinbacher collection)

F-104A msn 1025 with sidewinder rails on the wing tips. Notice the similarity in plan form of the horizontal stabilizer and the 104 wing. Lockheed built 153 F-104As. (Lockheed, Dave Steinbacher collection)

JF-104

NASA or USAF typically used a "J" prefix for a temporary modification to an aircraft. Usually these modifications could be undone to return the aircraft to its original configuration.

NF-104A

Lockheed modified three F-104As for the USAF as aerospace trainers. Major difference was the 6,000-pound thrust rocket in the tail, extended wing tips and the addition of reaction jet controls. See chapter 7 for further details.

QF-104A

Lockheed and Sperry Phoenix modified twenty-four YF-104As and F-104As in 1959 to 1960 as high-speed target drones. Externally they were the same as the F104As, with remote flight control equipment installed internally. These target drones flew from late 1960 until the early 1970s.

One of 24 QF-104As used as high-speed target drones. The bright orange paint scheme made it easy to identify the radio-controlled target. The remote control system did not interfere with the ability to use a pilot in the aircraft for checkout and ferry flights. (Lockheed, via Tony Landis)

Early photo of YF-104A number 17, USAF s/n 55-2971. The YF-104 did not have a ventral fin at this stage. A total of 17 YF models were built for production prototype testing. They had a lengthened fuselage and the higher-thrust J79-GE-3A engine. The new supersonic conical inlets were first used for the YF-104As. All succeeding models had the conical inlets. (Lockheed, Dave Steinbacher collection)

F-104B

Lockheed built 26 F-104Bs, which were two-seat versions of the F-104A. The F-104B had the same engine and Mach 2.0 performance as the F-104A. Overall dimensions were also the same as in the 'A' model. Empty weight was up slightly at 12,866 pounds, and the maximum take-off gross weight was 23,535 pounds. The 'B' model did not have the M-61 Vulcan gun, but it did have four stores pylons and the normal AN/ASG-14T1 fire control system.

Rocket power, in addition to the standard J79 engine, gave the NF-104A the ability to fly to altitudes of 120,000 feet. In addition to the 6,000-pound thrust rocket in the tail, extended wing tips and reaction controls for the high altitude operation were added to three F-104As in the modifications performed by Lockheed. (Lockheed, Jim Upton collection)

Number two F-104B with tip tanks installed. Armament on the 104B included four stores pylons and the AN/ASG-14T1 fire control system. 'B' model did not have the M-61 Vulcan gun, even though the covered gun port is visible in this photo. Space for the ammo boxes was eliminated with the second seat installation. (Lockheed, Dave Steinbacher collection)

Lockheed built 26 F 104Bs, which were a two-seat version of the F 104A. The F-104B had the same engine and Mach 2.0 performance of the F-104A. Overall dimensions were also the same as the 'A' model. (Lockheed, Dave Steinbacher collection)

F-104C

Lockheed built 77 F-104C all-weather fighter-bombers for USAF Tactical Air Command. The "C" differed from earlier versions as it featured in-flight refueling capability using a removable probe on the left side of the fuselage. The F-104C first flew on 24 July 1958. Blown flaps (BLC) were added to improve take-off and landing performance. The "C" models had the J79-GE-7 engine, which produced 10,000 pounds of static thrust and 15,800 pounds of thrust in afterburner. Range was 1,642 nautical miles with tip tanks and pylon tank (dropping the pylon tank when it was empty). Empty weight was 12,526 pounds and maximum take-off gross weight was 27,537 pounds.

By early 1963, operational problems had resulted in 40 serious incidents and the loss of 24 aircraft and nine pilots. Most of these were related to problems with the J79-GE-7 engines. A modification program by General Electric, which corrected the problem, was started in May 1963 and completed in June 1964.

Weapons on the F-104C includ-

QF-104 USAF 60739 taxis out without a pilot on board. The pilots are on top of the mobile control vehicle to the right. F-104A msn 1027 was the 8th F-104A built and was later modified to the "QF" radio controlled drone configuration. (Lockheed Martin)

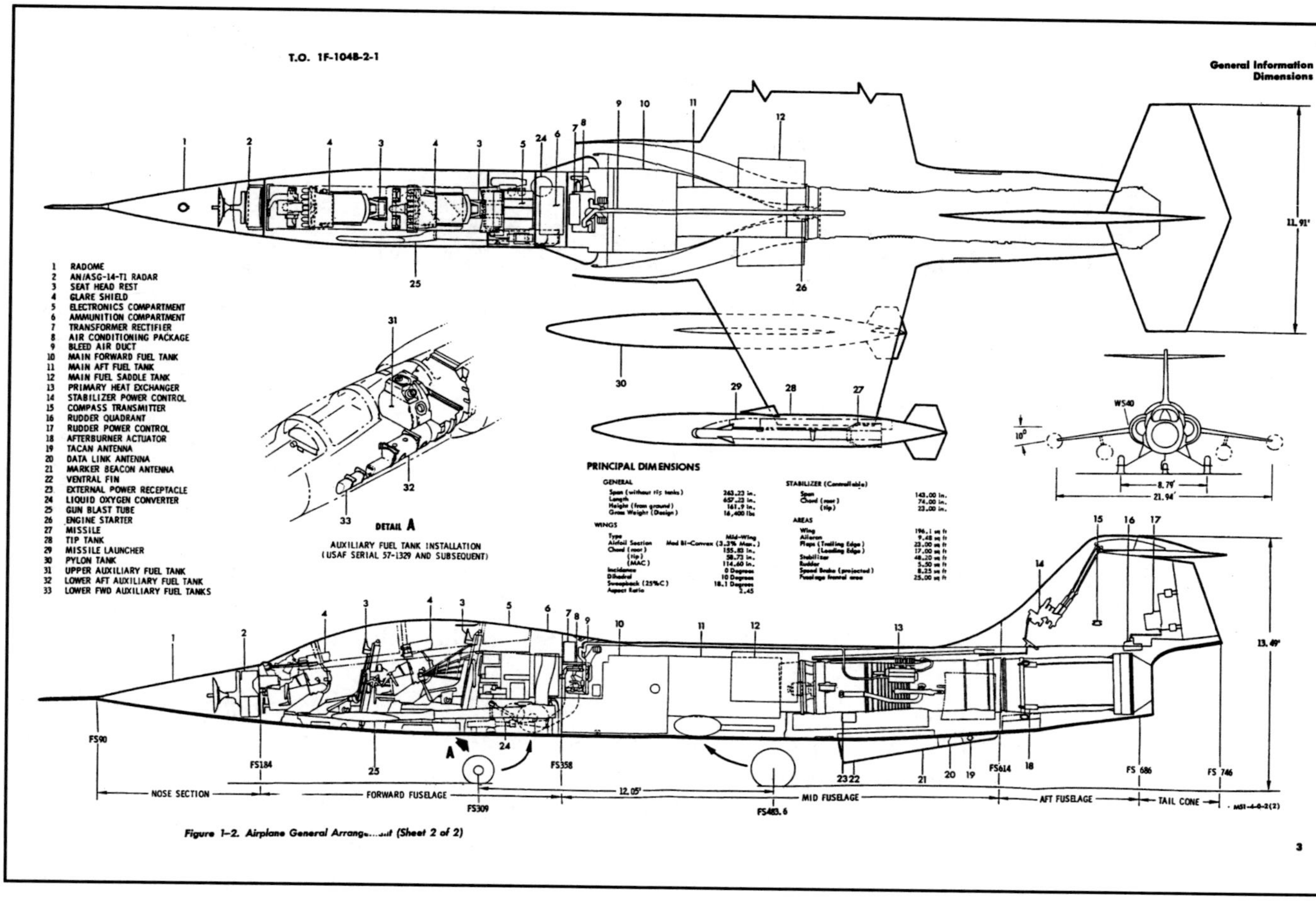

Cutaway view of the Lockheed two-place F-104B. Some of the changes to the F-104 for the two-place models included retracting the nose landing gear aft and using the Gatling gun space for auxiliary fuel tanks. Dimensions and performance were the same as the "A" model. (John Whittenbury collection)

ed the 20-mm Vulcan cannon and four pylons for AIM-9 Sidewinder missiles, with two on the wing tips and two on fuselage pylons. The craft could carry bombs and unguided 2.75-inch rockets on under-wing and fuselage stations. Fire control system was the AN/ASG-14T-2.

F-104B msn 5015, USAF 57-1303, on the Edwards AFB lakebed 30 December 1954 was the 15th 'B' model built. Performance and dimensions of the two-seat 'B' model was essentially the same as the 'A' model. Notice the NASA markings on the tail in addition to the USAF markings. (NASA Dryden via Tony Landis)

F-104D

Twenty-one F-104Ds, a two-seat version of the F-104C, were built by Lockheed, the first of which flew on 31 October 1958. The 'D' had the same engine as the F-104C and maximum speed was Mach 2.0. Range was 1388 nautical miles, with tip tanks and pylon tank (dropping the pylon tank when it was empty).

F-104C was an all-weather fighter-bomber for USAF Tactical Air Command. Differences from the F-104A included addition of a removable probe on the left side of the fuselage for aerial refueling. The F-104C first flew on 24 July 1958. Blown flaps (BLC) were added improving takeoff and landing performance. (Lockheed, Dave Steinbacher collection)

Empty weight was 13,073 pounds and maximum take-off gross weight was 24,388 pounds. The 'D' model did not have the M-61 Gatling gun, but did have five stores pylons and the AN/ASG-14 fire control system. Like the 'B' model, the nose gear retracted aft and the larger vertical fin was incorporated.

F-104DJ

Lockheed and Mitsubishi built 20 two-place F-104DJs. The "DJ," version of the F-104D for the Japanese ASDF (Air Self Defense Force), was equipped with the J79-GE-11A engine with 15,800 pounds thrust in afterburner. Performance was essentially the same as the F-104D. The F-104DJ had five pylons and no M-61 Gatling gun.

F-104F

Lockheed built 30 two-place F-104Fs for the West German Air Force. The F-104F was a version of the F-104D equipped to F-104G standards. Engine was the J79-GE-7 and performance was essentially the same as the F-104D. There were five external store stations and no M-61 Gatling gun. Primary use was as a transition trainer for converting to supersonic fighter-bombers.

F-104C with the leading edge flaps down, slowing for the photo aircraft. Weapons on the F-104C included the 20-mm Vulcan cannon, four pylons for AIM-9 Sidewinder missiles, bombs and unguided 2.75-inch rockets. The F-104C won the 1962 Fighter Weapons Meet as the only F-104 against 13 competitors. (Lockheed, Dave Steinbacher collection)

F-104G Super Starfighter

An all-weather fighter-bomber version of the F-104C, the F-104G was the model with the largest production run. A total of 1,127 F-104Gs were manufactured by seven different companies.

Companies included Lockheed in the USA, Canadair in Canada, Fiat in Italy, Fokker in the Netherlands, MBB and Messerschmitt in Germany, Mitsubishi in Japan and SABCA-Fairy in Belgium. This turned out to be the greatest international cooperative venture in the history of the aerospace business.

The F-104G differed from the F-104C in its reinforced structure, larger tail surface area with fully powered rudder as used on the two-seat Starfighters and combat maneuvering flaps. Avionics were vastly improved, centered around the Autonetics F15A NASARR (North American Search And Ranging Radar) fire control system and featuring a larger weapons load capacity. The Lockheed C-2 upward-firing ejection seat delivered with the aircraft was gradually phased out in favor of the Martin-Baker "zero-zero" seat, which meant that ejection could be accomplished at zero altitude above the ground and at zero airspeed.

The F-104G had the J79-GE-11A engine, which produced 15,600 pounds of thrust. Maximum speed was Mach 2.2 and range was 1628 nautical miles with tip tanks and pylon tank. Empty weight was 13,592 pounds, and maximum Take-Off Gross Weight was 28,580 pounds. The F-104G had five pylons, one on the fuselage and four on the wings. Dimensions of the 'G' model are the same as the F-104A and 'C' models. Navigation system included the Litton LN-3 inertial navigator.

Weapons on the F-104G included the M61 Vulcan Cannon, four pylons for Sidewinder missiles, as well as the NASARR system to provide radar search, acquisition, and automatic tracking for lead-collision or lead-pursuit attack with missiles. The bombing computer was linked with the inertial navigator, air-data computer, and the NASARR fire control system. First flight of the F-104G was at Lockheed Palmdale on 7 June 1960, and the final F-104G was delivered by MBB in 1973 — a very long production run.

Danish F-104D, photographed in 1978. Lockheed built 21 F-104Ds as a two-seat version of the F-104C. The 'D' first flew on October 31, 1958 with the same engine as the F-104C and maximum speed was Mach 2.0. The 'D' model did not have the M-61 Gatling gun, but had five stores pylons and the AN/ASG-14 fire control system. Like the 'B' model, the nose gear retracted aft and the larger vertical fin was incorporated. (MAP)

TF-104G

These were a two-seat version of the F-104G built by Lockheed. They were combat-ready aircraft and not just trainers. Performance was essentially the same as the F-104G. Weapons system included the TF-15A NASARR fire control system, LN-3 inertial navigation system, and four external stores stations.

RF-104G

This was a tactical reconnaissance version of the F-104G. Aircraft were almost identical to the F-104G. Several reconnaissance systems were used. Some had all internal cameras, usually carrying three KS-67A cameras in the nose. The Vulcan cannon and magazine were removed for space with the internal installations. Others had flat-sided fixed ventral pods on the centerline fuselage, and some had round

West German Air Force two-place F-104F taxis for take-off. This was a version of the F-104D equipped to F-104G standards. Lockheed built 30 for the WGAF, which used it primarily as a transition trainer for converting to the F-104Gs. (MAP)

The F-104G was an all-weather fighter-bomber version of the F-104C. It was the model with the largest production run. A total of 1127 F-104Gs were built by seven different companies in seven countries. Here msn 2024 climbs above the California desert. Lockheed-built F-104Gs initially carried USAF markings until delivery, and a number of these were based at Luke Air Force Base, Arizona, where pilot training was held for the West German Air Force. (Lockheed, Dave Steinbacher collection)

removal pods on the fuselage. Lockheed built 40 RF-104Gs, Fokker built 119, and Fiat built 30. A lot of RF-104Gs were later modified to F-104Gs.

CF-104

The CF-104 was the Canadian interceptor version of the F-104G. Two hundred CF-104s were built by Canadair. Performance and dimensions were the same as the F-104G. Weapon systems included R-24A NASARR fire control system, M-61 Gatling gun and five external stores stations. Engine was the licensed-built J79-OEL-7 with 15,800 pounds thrust in afterburner. It was also fitted with a removable refueling probe.

F-104G with fuselage sidewinder rails. Compared to the F-104C, the F-104G had a reinforced structure, larger tail surface area with fully powered rudder as used on the two-seat Starfighters, combat maneuvering flaps, and vastly improved avionics centered around the Autonetics F15A NASARR, and a larger weapons load capacity. (Lockheed, Dave Steinbacher collection)

CF-104D

This model was a two-seat version of the CF-104. Lockheed built 38 of the units for the Canadian Forces. Empty weight was 13,999 pounds and maximum take-off gross weight was 27,215 pounds. Performance was essentially the same as the CF-104. Weapons systems included the R-24A NASARR fire control system, no M-61 Gatling gun and 5 external stores stations.

F-104J

The F-104J was a version of the F-104G built for the Japanese ASDF. Lockheed built the first three, Mitsubishi assembled the next 29 from Lockheed supplied parts, and the subsequent 177 were built by Mitsubishi. Performance was essentially the same as the F-104G. Weapons system included the F-15J NASARR fire control system and five external stores stations.

F-104N

Lockheed built three 'N' models in the F-104G configuration for NASA supersonic chase and research aircraft. All military systems — like the fire control system and weapons like the Gatling gun — were not installed in this model, freeing up space for NASA equipment. The F-104N is not to be confused with the NF-104A, which was a Lockheed modification that included a rocket in the tail for three aerospace trainers.

F-104S

The F-104S was the last version built of the F-104. Two F-104S prototypes were modified from Italian F-104Gs by Lockheed and 245 'S' models were built by Fiat in Italy for use by Italy and Turkey as an advanced all-purpose aircraft with improved capability as an interceptor and as a fighter-bomber. As an interceptor it had an R21G NASARR fire control radar, two AIM-7 Sparrow II, missiles and two AIM-9 Sidewinder missiles.

The first Lockheed-modified F-104S flew in December 1966, and Fiat went on to produce 245 'S' models. Fiat deliveries ran from December 1968 until March 1979. A modernized F-104S ASA (Updated Weapons System) flew with a look down/shoot- down radar, Selenia Aspide 1A air-to-air missiles and modern ECM (Electronic Counter Measures) systems flew in December 1984. Most remaining Italian F-104S models were upgraded to this configuration.

Dimensions are the same on the F-104S as the other production model F-104s, but there are significant differences in the 'S' model. The engine has the much higher thrust J79-GE-19, with 11,800 pounds and 17,900 pounds thrust in afterburner. Maximum speed is Mach 2.2, and range is 1588 nautical miles. Maximum altitude is over 60,000 feet. Empty weight is 14,753 pounds and maximum Take-Off Gross Weight is 31,000 pounds. In the fighter-bomber role, the S-model has the 20-mm Vulcan and up to 7,500 pounds of bombs, napalm tanks, or rocket pods on nine external attach points, the largest number of pylons on any F-104 model. It carries one pylon at the fuselage centerline, two on the outer fuselage, four on the wings and two on the wing tips. Fire control system includes the R21G NASARR. Navigation equipment includes the Litton LN-3 inertial navigator.

The 'S' model can be visually distinguished from other F-104 models by the two strakes on the lower

F-104G msn 2020 on take-off from Lockheed Palmdale. The J79-GE-11A engine produced 15,600 pounds of thrust. Maximum speed was Mach 2.2, and range was 1628 nautical miles with tip tanks and pylon tank. The 'G' model was sometimes referred to as the Super F-104. (Lockheed, Dave Steinbacher collection)

Two-place F-104DJ is the third aircraft down the line of Japan's F-104s. Lockheed and Mitsubishi built 22 two-place F-104DJs, which essentially had the performance of the F-104D. These were for the Japanese ASDF (Air Self-Defense Force). Weapon capability was the same as the F-104D. (Lockheed, Dave Steinbacher collection)

CF-104 is the Canadian interceptor version of the F-104G. Two hundred CF-104s were built by Canadair. Performance and dimensions were the same as the F-104G. (Lockheed, Dave Steinbacher collection)

RF-104G msn 4024. Tactical reconnaissance versions were almost identical to the F-104G. Several reconnaissance systems were used. Some had all internal cameras, usually carrying three KS-67A cameras in the nose. (Lockheed, Jim Upton collection.)

aft fuselage. Strakes were added during flight-testing to increase directional stability at speeds above Mach 2.0.

The Italian Air Force is still flying the F-104S in 2003 as their primary air defense aircraft. Alenia finished upgrading the F-104S models at the end of 2002 to the F-104S ASAM configuration, which is intended to keep the Starfighter in operation until it is replaced by the Eurofighter Typhoon, probably in 2004 or beyond. A fighter aircraft that started flying as the XF-104 in March 1954 evolved through the F-104S and is still flying today.

Italian F-104S on landing. The 'S' model can be visually distinguished from other F-104 models by the two strakes on the lower aft fuselage. The engine is the much higher thrust J79-GE-19, with 17,900 pounds thrust in afterburner. Maximum speed is Mach 2.2. This was the last version of the F-104 built. The 'S' model has nine external store stations, the largest number of all the F-104 models. Italian Air Force F-104S aircraft were still flying in 2003. (Lockheed, Dave Steinbacher collection)

Weapons Systems 5

Gatling Gun, Bombing Systems, and Missiles

Initially designed as an interceptor, the Lockheed F-104 Starfighter ended up carrying a large variety of weapons after its conversion to a low-level strike aircraft. In this role, options included a Vulcan M-61 cannon, Sidewinder missiles, 19 folding-fin 2.75-inch air-to-air rockets at mid-wing pylon stations, and GAM 83 air-to-ground missiles mounted at each wing pylon station. A variety of bombs and other stores were mounted on either wing pylon racks or beneath the fuselage on a center-line rack.

Gatling Gun

The F-104 was the first fighter to use the rapid-fire 20-mm Vulcan cannon, often referred to as a Gatling gun. Today, many USAF fighter and attack aircraft continue to use the Gatling gun, including the McDonnell-Douglas F-15, General Dynamics F-16, Fairchild A-10, and the Lockheed Martin F-22. A lot of the early development problems in using the rapid-fire cannon in a fighter aircraft were solved during the development of the F-104 and started with the XF-104. Development of this gun was very important for the F-104 program, and when one of the two XF-104s was lost during a gun-firing test, part of the gun development continued in a modified Lockheed YF-94D Starfire.

The M-61 Vulcan cannon, named after the Roman god of fire, was claimed at the time to be the world's fastest-firing gun of its type. The M-61 had six 20-mm barrels and a maximum firing rate of 6,000 rounds per minute — a whopping 100 rounds a second. The barrels rotated about the gun's longitudinal axis when firing. General Electric initially developed the gun.

The Vulcan design borrowed two features from the famous Gatling gun, which, patented in 1862, was a significant weapon in the American civil war. Both had a rotating cluster of barrels, and both were driven externally. In modern contrast to the hand crank that turned the Gatling, the Vulcan could use either hydraulic or electrical power. Lockheed chose to go electric. The gun weighed 300 pounds and was 72 inches long.

Ammunition was supplied by one feeder system. Rotating counterclockwise, the cannon fired at the nine o'clock position, with cartridges ejected at the four o'clock position and new rounds picked up at the two o'clock position. Successive rounds were fired independently of the previous round and dud rounds were ejected automatically.

The M-61 Vulcan was fired by a trigger on the pilot's control stick. Belted ammunition was stored in a

Old and new. The M-61 Vulcan 20-mm cannon on the right borrowed two features from the famous Gatling gun on the left, which, though patented in 1862, was a significant weapon in the American Civil War. Both had a rotating cluster of barrels, and they were driven externally. In modern contrast to the hand crank that turned the Gatling, the Vulcan can use either hydraulic or electrical power. Lockheed chose to go electric. The Vulcan's rate of fire is an astounding 6,000 rounds a minute. The Civil War uniform is also an interesting contrast with the partial pressure suit of the F-104 pilot. (Lockheed, Dave Steinbacher collection)

The Vulcan cannon is mounted in the lower left side of the fuselage. Gun opening can be seen below the cockpit on this YF-104A. Vulcan cannon testing started on the XF-104, which was the first fighter to fly this advanced gun. (Lockheed, Dave Steinbacher collection)

box located behind the cockpit. At 6,000 rounds per minute, all the actions of the air-cooled Vulcan were virtually simultaneous.

The gun is installed in a fixed position in the forward left side of the aircraft's lower fuselage. The ammunition container is located above the gun, just aft of the electronics compartment. The M-61 gun is electrically driven by 208 volt AC power. The 20-mm cartridges are fired electrically. Each round fired is counted electronically, and the total number of remaining rounds is displayed on a Veeder-Root-type counter on the cockpit armament control panel. After a round is fired, the empty case is stowed in a compartment below the gun, and the links are jettisoned.

Weapon Selection

A selector switch allows the pilot to select gun, missiles, rocket or bomb drop mode, and to choose from which armament station the weapon will be fired or dropped. Pressing the trigger on the top of the control stick fires forward-firing weapons. Bombs are released by pressing the external stores release (pickle) button on the control stick. A bomb fuse-arming switch controls fuse-arming wires so that bombs can either be dropped armed or jettisoned safe. The Sidewinder firing circuits are interconnected so that one missile is fired per single trigger pull, so that up to four Sidewinders may be pre-selected for sequence firing by separate and distinct trigger pulls.

Stores may be jettisoned in flight from any or all external stations. The jettison system operates the normal

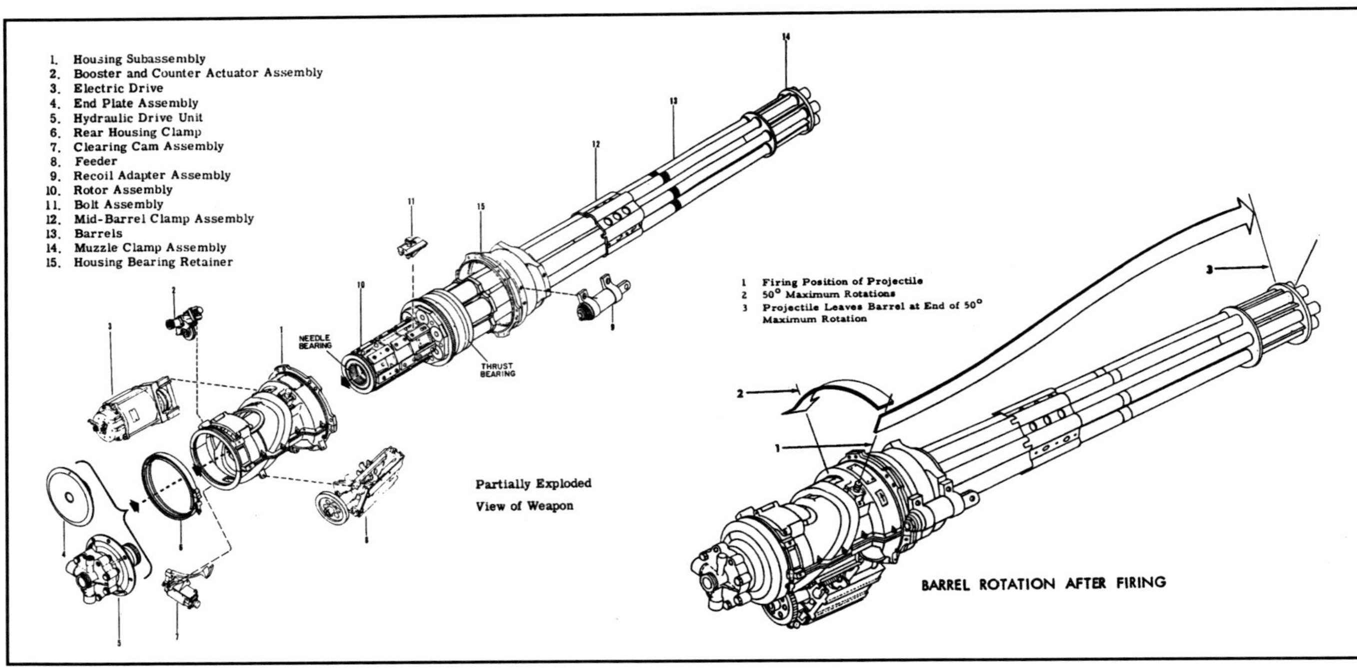

This diagram shows the Starfighter's rotating gun barrels of the M-61 20-mm rapid-fire cannon. This gun will fire 6,000 rounds per minute! (Lockheed, Bill Nickloff collection)

This illustrates M-61 Cannon installation in the F-104, showing location of the blast tube on the side of the fuselage and the ammunition box. (Lockheed, Bill Nickloff collection)

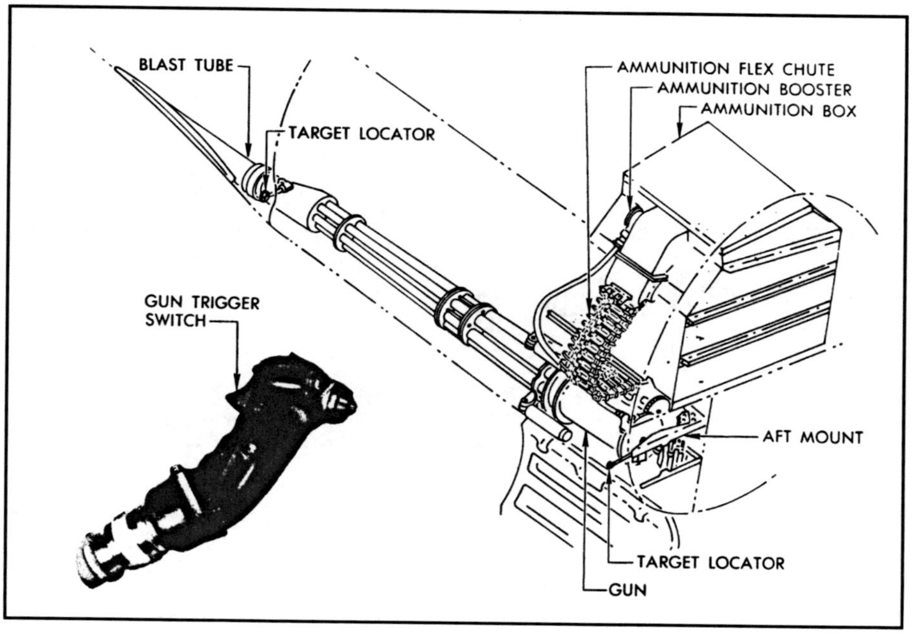

drop system for each station. When bombs are jettisoned they will fall armed or safe as previously selected with the arming switch. Actuation of an emergency switch will jettison all external stores except a centerline bomb. The centerline bomb must be jettisoned separately because of special weapons that may be carried at this station.

Bombing Systems

Center-line rack on the F-104 could accommodate standard bombs of all sizes up to 2,000 pounds, as well as nuclear weapons. Wing pylon racks could haul general-purpose bombs up to 1,000 pounds. The Starfighter had true high-speed bombing capability, due to its use of electrical weapons arming. Without electrical arming, supersonic aircraft's bombs were armed mechanically in a fashion similar to what had been used in World War II. This restricted aircraft to dropping their stores sub-sonically because the mechanical linkage between the bomb and the aircraft tended to fly loose at supersonic speeds.

M-2 System

The M-2 Bombing System, with inputs from the Air Data Computer, inertial navigator and radar fire control system, permitted delivery of

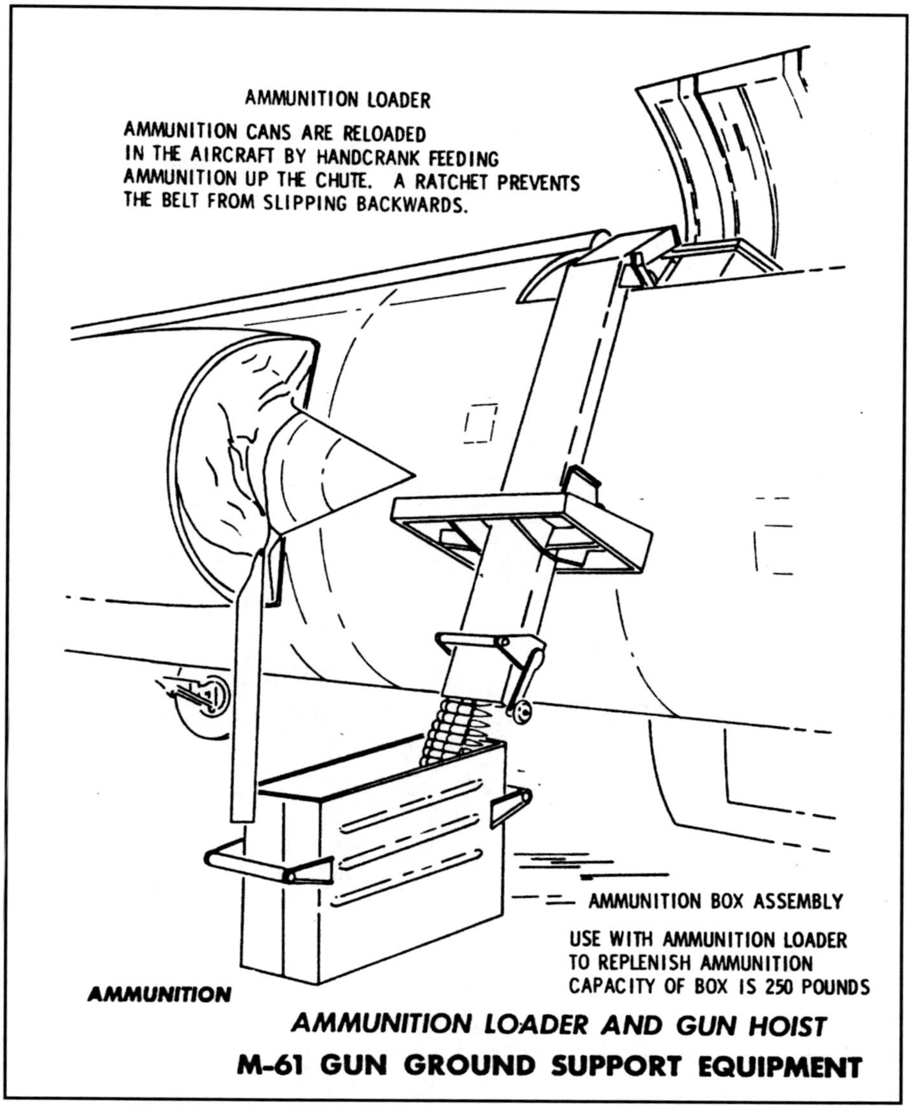

Ground servicing and loading 20-mm ammunition into the 104 for the M-61 Vulcan rapid-fire cannon. Ammunition cans are reloaded by hand-crank feeding ammo up the chute. (Lockheed, Bill Nickloff collection)

Sidewinder air-to-air missiles, along with the M-61 Vulcan cannon, were the primary weapons for the interceptor-configured F-104s. F-104A, msn 1036, is shown on a test flight over the Antelope Valley near Palmdale. (Lockheed, Dave Steinbacher collection)

conventional and special (nuclear) weapons using any one of eight techniques: Dive toss, high dive toss; low loft; level approach low loft; level approach high loft; over-the-shoulder; level approach low altitude; level approach, high altitude, high cruise; and level approach, high altitude, high speed.

Blind bombing from level flight, because of clouds or darkness, could be conducted by using the ground map mode of the radar system. Variables affecting the delivery, such as weapon ballistics, identification point distance, wind velocity and direction, and type of burst were set into the bombing system control panel.

Dual Timer Bombing Method

A dual timer could be substituted for the M-2 bombing computer. It was a simple, reliable aid for release of either free-fall or retarded stores against known targets.

This bombing technique allowed a semi-automatic way to deliver a weapon at high speed and perform an escape maneuver at the earliest possible time in the weapon delivery. The dual timer installation in the F-104 consisted of a run-in timer and a release timer. When a mission was performed using the dual timer system, attack maneuver was completely programmed. The calculated timer settings were dependent on the Initial Point (IP) to target distance, speed and altitude of approach, and the pull-up maneuver planned. The accuracy of the system was dependent on the calculated timer setting and the pilot's ability to fly the programmed attack maneuver. The run-in timer was preset to the calculated time required to fly from the selected initial point to the planned pull-up point. When the run-in cycle was completed, the pilot would initiate the pull-up maneuver. The release timer automatically started when the run-in timer cycle was completed. The release timer setting was calculated to release the weapon at a specific point in the programmer pull-up to obtain a target hit. When the release cycle was completed, the weapon was released.

The Initial Point or Identification Point where the bomb button is actuated can be determined in three ways:

1. By an IP with a known distance from the target.
2. By using the optical sight.
3. By using radar in the ground map mode to determine target distance.

F-104C at George Air Force Base, California, displays some of the weapons the F-104 can carry. Weapons shown include the Vulcan 20-mm cannon; sidewinder air-air missiles; 2.75-inch rockets; demolition bombs, fire bombs, and a nuclear weapon practice unit. For an aircraft that started as a fighter-interceptor, the F-104 grew to combination fighter-bomber. (Lockheed, Dave Steinbacher collection)

The Super Starfighter (F-104G) was given a new bombing computer which, tied in with the inertial navigator, air data computer and the NASARR system, automated the relationship between the bomb trajectory and the aircraft in three dimensional space. Using this system, bomb release could be relied upon to take place at the exact point in space to impact on the target. With the computer, the pilot had a choice of several basic bomb delivery methods, including pull-up and release and run-in and release. Such methods could make use of the director sight, the NASARR radar, or just the "Mark I eyeball."

Ground crew loading 2.75-inch rockets into the LAU-3A rocket launcher on the F-104. The LAU-3A launcher carried 19 rockets and the 104 could carry multiple launcher pods. (Lockheed, Dave Steinbacher collection)

Azimuth Offset Bomb Delivery

A pilot could use the F-104's radar to deliver a weapon on a target that may not be visible, such as an underground target. Using a known radar reference point up to 40,000 feet to the left or right of the target, a parallel offset course could be flown. The azimuth-offset cursor on the radar displayed the selected offset as a center cursor for the pilot to fly to the target.

Fire Control System

The Starfighter's multipurpose radar system supplied guidance information for air-to-air and air-to-ground attack against targets that could not be seen by the pilot. It also provided cockpit displays for ground mapping, contour mapping, and terrain avoidance as an aid to navigation. This permitted low-altitude intrusions at night or during bad weather.

To meet the mission requirements of the customer countries, F-104 fire-control systems were essentially tailor-made for each version of the aircraft. At the heart of the system was North American Search and Ranging Radar (NASARR). This was the Starfighter's "aiming brain." It consisted of a radar set incorporating an optional fire control computer. The equipment operated in two basic modes: air-to-ground, for bombing and navigation; and air-to-air, for target interception. It was capable of providing data link information read-out from a ground station.

In its air-to-ground mode, the NASARR system provided ranging information for bombing computation in visual bombing situations; ground mapping for navigation; and terrain-avoidance for flying low-level approaches to the operational zone.

In the air-to-air mode, NASARR and its fire control computer provided radar search and acquisition and automatic tracking of air targets for lead-collision attacks and the automatic release of missiles. In lead-pursuit attacks, using the Vulcan gun or missiles, the fire control computer provided information to the director type gun sight. The armament control computer produced a steering dot on the radarscope that

F-104C 57-0930 takes off with two LAU-3A rocket launchers on the wing pylons. (Lockheed, Dave Steinbacher collection)

Four F-104Cs of the Tactical Air Command in formation carrying 2000-pound bombs. (Lockheed, Dave Steinbacher collection)

enabled the pilot to maneuver the aircraft into a firing position.

Optical and IR Sight System

The director gun sight gave the pilot an optical indication of the line of sight with the proper lead angle for firing, as computed by the NASARR fire control computer. When caged (or fixed), the sight could be used as an aiming reference for firing missiles in pursuit attack, and these capabilities could be used at night as well by using an infra-red sight. In addition, the caged sight could be used as an aiming reference for visual dive-bombing attacks. The gun-sight camera photographs the sight picture through an optical periscope.

The sight system projected a reticle and movable target dot onto the combining glass, allowing the pilot to maneuver the aircraft to superimpose the dot on the target. The armament control computer automatically computed the correct lead for the gun. The infrared tracking sight was also projected on the combining glass, enabling targets to be tracked without visual reference, as in the dark of night.

Ground Controlled Intercept

The GCI equipment displayed data linked from a ground radar station to the cockpit display.

Later-model F-104s were equipped with the Time Division Data Link (TDDL) that helped guide the pilot to his target. This equipment provided a means of receiving course direction, computed at the ground radar station, until acquisi-

F-104S with mockup Sparrow missiles on the outboard pylons and sidewinders on the inboard pylons. (Lockheed, Dave Steinbacher collection)

tion was made by the fighter's own NASARR radar. The system could be used for either an air defense or ground support mission, providing the pilot with a visual display of his intercept situation and providing a "return-to-base" function. The TDDL eliminated "language barriers" such as static or other interference associated with voice transmissions. It also stored in memory the latest received information and permitted a selective addressing so that many fighters could operate from one ground radar station. TDDL provided a high degree of invulnerability to jamming and made it possible for the more powerful ground radar station's target information to be presented on the pilot's radar indicator.

UHF Communications

Super Starfighters had an improved ultra high frequency (UHF) command communication set as part of their advanced electronics equipment. The new UHF gear was lighter than its predecessor's, requiring about 500 cubic inches less space when repackaged in "jeep cans" for location in the integrated electronics compartment. The jeep can was a packaged box or unit containing various electronics items. Each was shaped to fit precisely into the electronics compartment. They all had the same height and depth, but could vary in width. Each had a self-test facility that allowed rapid "go, no-go" check-out after it had been installed in the aircraft.

Reconnaissance System

Several photo reconnaissance systems were developed for the Starfighter. Among them were two external camera pod systems and two versions of an internally mounted camera system. A large camera pod system was developed for high- and low-altitude reconnaissance, and a smaller pod, mounting cameras of smaller format and shorter focal length, was developed for reconnaissance at lower altitudes. The internal camera systems used three 70 mm format cameras with normal focal length lenses for low-to-medium altitude reconnaissance. The differences in the two internal systems were minor from a functional point of view, relating mostly to camera types used. Some Starfighters had an increased internal fuel capacity when the cameras were installed. This was achieved by making modifications to accommodate the optional gun and ammunition bay fuel tanks

With the internal photo reconnaissance system installed, a fuselage centerline store and cameras could be carried simultaneously.

A WGAF F-104G fuselage-mounted reconnaissance pod during tests at Lockheed Palmdale in 1961. This large reconnaissance pod was developed for the Starfighter to provide a high-altitude reconnaissance capability. The pod accommodates a large-format camera with a long focal length lens. (Lockheed, Jim Fitzgerald collection)

Royal Canadian Air Force CF-104 with a reconnaissance pod at Lockheed Palmdale. The photo reconnaissance pod developed for the RCAF Starfighter accommodated a forward oblique camera and offered better angular coverage for the side oblique cameras than the internal system did. Like the internal system, this installation was primarily intended for low-altitude reconnaissance. (Lockheed, Jim Fitzgerald collection)

A formerly classified weapons test in the 1950s. A crane supported the F-104 and the trapeze-mounted MB-1 weapon was fired, breaking the frangible aerodynamic fairings. Approximately five aerial launches were made after the successful ground tests. The test was a Skunk Works project, and Henry Combs related that Kelly Johnson gave him 30 days to design, fabricate, and fire the weapon from the ground test fixture, which was accomplished. The first photo is before firing; the second photo shows the MB-1 at the moment of firing with the frangible fairing breaking. (Lockheed, Jim Upton collection)

This allowed the Starfighter to perform its own damage-assessment reconnaissance on an attack mission. Another advantage of the internal system was that it left the aircraft aerodynamically clean. There was no significant alteration to the external configuration that would allow ground observers to identify the Starfighter's mission.

The photo reconnaissance pod developed for the Royal Canadian Air Force accommodated a forward oblique camera and offered better angular coverage for the side oblique cameras than the internal system. Like the internal system, this installation was primarily intended for low-altitude reconnaissance.

Internal camera systems were used in F-104G aircraft. Three cameras were installed on a mounting rack in the expended ammunition case stowage compartment. The mounting rack moved vertically in the compartment to make camera servicing easier. A hinged door with optically flat windows was installed in the bottom of the compartment. The door had external power-actuated window covers so that the windows were protected during take-off and landing. One camera pointed vertically downward, one pointed obliquely to the right, and the other to the left.

The cameras included integral terrain light-sensing and automatic aperture control. A camera control was installed in the cockpit. Some systems included individual camera control. The 20-mm cannon was usually removed from reconnaissance aircraft while the cameras were installed, but the gun could be re-installed when the reconnaissance system was removed.

F-104S on take-off with a full load of weapons on all nine pylons! It is amazing what the F-104 can do with its stubby 7.5-foot wings. Notice the blow-in door opening aft of the engine inlets that provides additional airflow to the engine for take-off. (Lockheed, Dave Steinbacher collection)

Advanced Weapons Systems

The Lockheed XF-104 was the first fighter to use the rapid-fire 20-mm Vulcan cannon that is still used on many of today's current fighter and attack aircraft. The Starfighter was also the first to have supersonic bomb delivery capability. F-104 advanced fire control systems for air-to-air and air-to-ground systems also had an infrared sight system that could be used in the dark of

STARFIGHTER COLORS

1950s THROUGH 2003

The Lockheed F-104 Starfighter was probably 10 years ahead of its time when it made its first flight in 1954. This was only seven years after Chuck Yeager broke the sound barrier in the Bell X-1 rocket plane. Here was the start of an operational jet fighter that could fly, maneuver, and fight at twice the speed of sound using a single jet engine with a very advanced inlet system, small wing, and sophisticated weapons system. Over 16 models of the Starfighter were built with some exotic models like the NF-104 flying to the edge of space as an astronaut trainer and the ZELL model taking off without a runway. Fourteen free-world countries flew the F-104. The Italian-built F-104S models are still flying today as their primary air defense aircraft, and two civilian-owned CF-104s are currently flying 12-16 dynamic air shows annually throughout the United States and Canada.

This Lockheed Missiles and Space Company X-7, attached to its rocket booster assembly with vertical and horizontal stabilizer, is carried by a Boeing B-29 launch aircraft in 1952. This secret program was flown out of the Air Force Missile Development Center in Alamogordo, New Mexico. Crucial data for the F-104 design was obtained from these tests. The X-7 ultimately broke all altitude and speed records for air-breathing vehicles, reaching 106,000 feet and Mach 4.31. (Lockheed Martin)

F-104N number 812 on 16 June 1965 with a decelerator payload test shape mounted on the centerline store position. NASA 812 was one of three F-104N models built for NASA by Lockheed to F-104G standards.

An excellent view of the landing flaps on NASA 826 on landing approach over Edwards AFB lakebed. F-104 wing leading edge and trailing edge flaps increase the wing area and change the wing shape to optimize it for lower speed for landing. The trailing edge land flaps have Boundary Layer Control that improves the efficiency of the landing flaps lowering the landing speed of the F-104. (NASA)

An F-104 takes off without a runway! ZELL (ZEro Length Launch) was a secret Lockheed program at Edwards Air Force Base for the West German Air Force in 1963. Its purpose was to demonstrate the Starfighter's capability of carrying out combat operations without the use of runways for take-off. (Lockheed Martin)

ZELL (ZEro Length Launch) F-104 on the launch ramp before it is elevated to the launch position. (AFFTC)

The point-intercept air defense mission combines the requirements for high rates of climb, good acceleration, and high speed. Two Sidewinder-armed F-104As of the 83rd Fighter Interceptor Squadron fly over San Francisco bay. The 83rd FIS was based at McChord Air Force Base California. (Lockheed Martin)

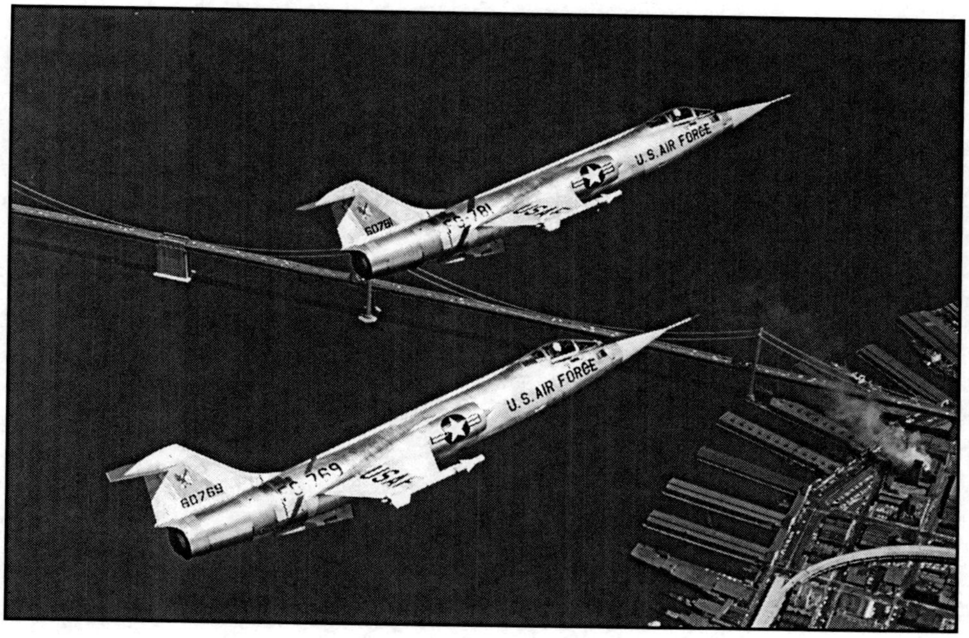

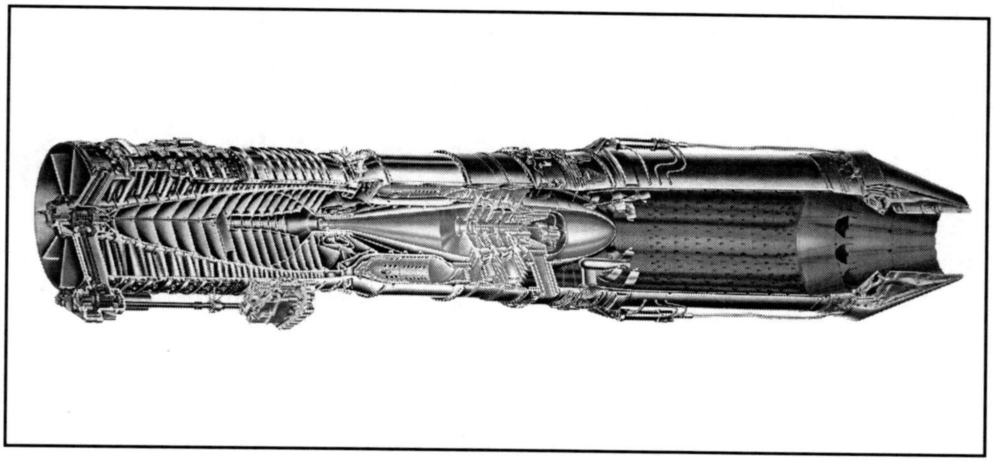

General Electric J79 axial flow, turbojet engine, with afterburner. Major components of the engine are, from left to right, a 17-stage compressor section, an accessory drive section; a combustion section, a three-stage turbine, a high-thrust afterburner, and a variable-area exhaust nozzle. (General Electric)

Ready for takeoff, Lockheed F-104A 60801 (msn 1089) was used as a supersonic chase aircraft for the secret Lockheed MD-21 program. Lockheed test pilot Art Peterson was flying chase for Bill Park in the M-21 (for Mother ship) in this early 1960s photo. The ramjet-powered D-21 drone was launched at Mach 3 speeds. Lockheed at one time studied a QF-104A drone for launch from the A-12. The F-104 s/n 60801 is now on a pole at the Edwards Air Force Base gym, and the MD-21 is in the Museum of Flight in Seattle Washington. (Lockheed via Tony Landis)

Lockheed NF-104A in a near vertical climb on 6 October 1964, with the Rocketdyne AR2-3 rocket engine at full thrust in addition to the thrust of the Starfighter's J79 engine. With the NF-104's reaction controls for high-altitude control, the NF-104A reached altitudes as high as 118,860 feet. (Lockheed Martin)

A rare combination: the Lockheed XF-104 Starfighter in formation flight with the other Century Series fighters, the Convair YF-102A Delta Dagger, McDonnell F-101A Voodoo, and the North American F-100A Super Sabre. The Starfighter is the lightest and fastest of the Century Series fighters. (AFFTC History Office via Tony Landis)

NASA 812, featuring a high-visibility, paint scheme, was one of three F-104Ns built for NASA by Lockheed to F-104G standards. (AFFTC)

The point-intercept air defense mission combines the requirements for high rates of climb, good acceleration, and high speed. The Starfighter configured as shown with Sidewinder missiles does this extremely well. YF-104A 52965 flying out of EAFB with wingtip mounted air-to-air Sidewinder missiles. (AFFTC)

QF-104A 52957 was originally the number three YF-104A. One of 24 F-104s converted to target drones, the QF-104As could be flown with or without a pilot in the cockpit. Typically a pilot in the cockpit was used for checkout and ferry flights. (Lockheed, Dave Steinbacher collection)

NASA 734 on the Edwards AFB lakebed on 16 November 1960. The instrumented nose cone on F-104 NASA 734 contained thermocouples, microphones, static orifices, boundary-layer microphone, and skin transmission-loss microphone. While the instrumented nose cone was fitted to F-104 NASA 734, the air data probe was placed at the wing tip of the left wing. (NASA Dryden via Tony Landis)

Japanese Air Self Defense Force (JASDF) F-104J on landing approach in 1973. Notice the dual-fuselage Sidewinder launch rails on the fuselage. Mitsubishi built 210 F-104Js. (MAP)

A Netherlands F-104G on landing approach in 1980, carrying two sidewinder air-to-air missiles. The Dutch Air Force had 95 F-104Gs. (MAP)

One of six F-104Bs delivered to the Jordanian Air Force, photographed in 1995. (MAP)

A two-place Italian F-104G(T), one of 24 in the Italian Air Force, photographed in 1981. The Italian Air Force also had 125 single-place F-104Gs and 205 F-104S models. (MAP)

Belgian F-104G in flight. The Belgian air force had a total of 100 F-104Gs. The emergency arresting hook is visible on the aft bottom fuselage. (MAP)

Italian F-104S on landing approach at the 1988 Tiger Meet. The striking Tiger Meet paint schemes were usually painted on with water-soluble paint. (MAP)

Dutch air force F-104G with an Oldelft Orpheus reconnaissance pod. Photograph was taken in 1976. (MAP)

Canadian Forces CF-104 on the ramp with a practice bomb dispenser on the centerline store position. (MAP)

Mark Sherman's CF-104D over the Arizona desert near home base at Williams Gateway Airport Phoenix. This is one of three known privately owned Starfighters currently flying. (via Mark Sherman)

"North American Eagle" is a racecar built from the fuselage of F-104A USAF s/n 56-763, with the purpose of setting a new land speed record. It was photographed in September 2002 near Pierce county airport in Washington with Mount Rainier in the background. (via Ed Shadle)

The curved secondary air-flow opening inside the right side inlet is very visible in this view of the "Svetkoff's Starfighters, Inc." CF-104D in 2000. The secondary airflow system is a key element in the inlet design, allowing excess air at supersonic speeds to pass through the engine compartment with minimum drag and be ejected past the secondary exit nozzle in a manner that improves exit nozzle efficiency. (Pete Clukey)

An interesting night shot of the Starfighters, Inc. CF-104 at NAS Jacksonville Naval Air Station in 1998. Starfighters, Inc. also has a two-place CF-104D, and this civilian team performs 12 to 16 dynamic airshows annually throughout the United States and Canada. (Pete Clukey)

OPERATORS 6 WORLDWIDE

STARFIGHTERS, USAF TO INTERNATIONAL

Naturally, given that they paid for the development of the aircraft, the United States was the first operator of the Starfighter. But many other countries would soon follow.

UNITED STATES

The first Lockheed XF-104 Starfighter was trucked to the Air Force Flight Test Center (AFFTC), Edwards AFB, California, on 25 February 1954 and flew on 4 March 1954. The YF-104A was tested at Edwards AFB beginning 17 February 1956. First operational F-104A in USAF service reached Hamilton AFB, California on 29 January 1958. Initially slated for Tactical Air Command (TAC) where it had been viewed as an F-100 Super Sabre replacement, the F-104A went to Air Defense Command (ADC) instead due to ADC's urgent need for an interceptor to fill in between the F-102 and F-106. The first F-104C for the USAF was accepted at George AFB, California on 15 October 1958. The first operational F-104D was accepted by the same squadron the following month.

In addition to the USAF, the US Navy also used three F-104s for Mach 2 supersonic launch development of the AIM-9 sidewinder missiles at their China Lake, California test facility.

One was a YF-104A and two were F-104As. The aircraft were on loan to the Navy but still crewed by Air Force Personnel. Aircraft wore Navy markings while at China Lake. Tests began in 1959 running through 1961.

In Action

USAF F-104A Starfighters from two squadrons from Hamilton AFB went into action for the first time from Nationalist Chinese and American bases on Formosa (Taiwan) in late 1958, following Chinese Communist aggression against the Republic of China island of Quemoy in the Straits of Formosa. The display of their Mach 2 capabilities recorded by PRC (Peoples Republic of China) ground radars proved a sufficient deterrent, although in reality most of the action was over by the time the Starfighters arrived, so their impact on Peking's leadership was negligible. In October 1961, when the USSR cut West German access links to Berlin, three Air National Guard F-104A squadrons assigned to Air Defense Command were transferred to Tactical Air Command and rushed to Europe to reinforce NATO's air defenses.

During the 1962 Cuban missile crisis, USAF F-104Cs were deployed to bases in the southeastern US as the most effective available counter to the threat of Soviet supplied MiG fighters operating from that island. They remained in that area until the late 1960s. Fifteen F-104Cs of the 479th Tactical Fighter Wing were also sent to South Vietnam in March

Two Lockheed USAF F-104As armed with sidewinder missiles fly formation with a Lockheed WV-2. The Air Force WV-2 was an airborne early-warning aircraft. Full of electronic gear, it had a crew of 32. (Lockheed, Dave Steinbacher collection)

USAF F-104A moves into refueling position behind a Boeing KB-50J tanker. (Lockheed, Dave Steinbacher collection)

F-104s were also refueled from Boeing KC-97s and KC-135s using a drogue basket adapter attached to the refueling boom. (Lockheed, Dave Steinbacher collection)

1965 to counter North Vietnamese interference with USAF strike aircraft, after MiG-17s of the North Vietnamese Air Force shot down two Republic F-105s. Each of the three F-104 squadrons served rotation tours, which were repeated in mid-1966, when the USAF still operated some 115 Starfighters. Included in the 115 were 40 F-104As at Homestead and Webb AFBs, and about 75 F-104Cs at George AFB. By early 1967 only one Starfighter squadron remained in the regular USAF inventory, and that one was finally disbanded a year later. F-104B/Cs continued operating with the Air National Guard until July 1975.

The USAF did not buy any F-104Gs, but they did operate a large number owned by the German air force based at Luke Air Force Base in Arizona. While most F-104Gs were built in Europe, Lockheed built 138 aircraft while the German Consortium was being set up.

Many of these 104s were used to establish the United States based Starfighter training program for German and NATO pilots. Round-the-year good weather was advantageous for training when compared to the weather conditions in Germany and other NATO countries. Starfighters used for training included both F-104G single-place and two-place F-104 models.

Four USAF F-104Cs in formation equipped with refueling probes. (Lockheed, Dave Steinbacher collection)

All F-104Gs used in the training program carried USAF markings while in the U.S., which explains why there are photos of USAF F-104Gs even though the USAF did not buy any 'G' models.

The USAF acquired the following number of aircraft:

2	XF-104 prototypes
17	YF-104 pre-production
153	F-104A
26	F-104B
77	F-104C
21	F-104D

International Operators

On duty with the air forces of 14 free world nations, the Mach 2 plus F-104 was a powerful persuader for peace. More than 2000 of the Lockheed-designed internationally–manufactured Starfighters were delivered to the air forces of Germany, Belgium, The Netherlands, Italy, Canada, Japan, Norway, Turkey, Greece, Nationalist China, Pakistan, Denmark, and Spain. The versatile stub-winged air superiority fighter/interceptor carried a varied multi-mission arsenal, including rockets, bombs, missiles and the world's fastest firing aerial cannon, the M-61 Vulcan. Seven countries produced the Starfighters in aviation's largest international aircraft program.

F-104C at George AFB, California is decked in camouflage paint in preparation for deployment to Vietnam. The refueling probe is installed and the pilot checks the M-61 Vulcan canon at the open hatch. (Lockheed, Dave Steinbacher collection)

Belgium

SABCA's share in the European Starfighter production program involved licensed construction of 100 F-104Gs for Belgium and 88 F-104Gs for Germany starting in 1963. Delivery of the first SABCA-built aircraft took place on 14 February 1963. Belgian production was completed in mid-1965. An F-104G and a TF-104G made the last formal Starfighter flights on 19 September 1983.

Belgium acquired the following number of aircraft:

100 F-104G
12 TF-104G

Canada

Canadair Ltd built 200 CF-104 versions of the F-104G for the Royal Canadian Air Force (RCAF) (now Canadian Forces) after Lockheed's prototype conversion. The first was rolled out from Cartierville in Montreal on 18 March 1961, before making its initial flight at Palmdale 10 days later. Powered by the Orenda-built J79-OEL-7 turbojet developing 10,000-pound military thrust, and 15,800 pounds with afterburning, the CF-104 was virtually identical to the F-104G. However, all but the two tactical

"Super Starfighters" referred to the 'G' variants of the F-104 with the higher-thrust General Electric J79-GE-11A engine and Mach 2.2 performance. Fourteen countries operated Super Starfighters. (Lockheed, Dave Steinbacher collection)

Five Canadian Forces CF-104s in formation flight. These were the first five of 200 CF-104s built by Canadair. (Lockheed, Dave Steinbacher collection)

One of 12 Belgian TF-104Gs with wing-tip fuel tanks and two pylon stores. (MAP)

Canadian CF-104 on landing approach. One of two Radar Airborne Warning blisters is visible at the tail cone and the Electronic Countermeasures (ECM) blister is visible under the nose radome. (MAP)

reconnaissance squadrons of Number 1 Wing were intended for nuclear roles, so the Canadian Starfighters had 1,000 pounds of additional fuel in place of the normal 20-mm Vulcan cannon. These were later installed when the CF-104s relinquished their nuclear role in January 1972 in favor of conventional ground attack, for which they also received twin bomb ejector rack carriers and multi-tube rocket-launchers. RCAF Starfighter orders also included 38 Lockheed built two-seat CF-104D trainers, the first of which made its initial flight at Palmdale on 14 June 1961.

Canadair received US-funded Mutual Aid orders for another 140 Starfighters to F-104G standards, mainly for Greece, Taiwan and Turkey, as well as Denmark, Norway and Spain. The last were delivered in September 1966.

Canadian Starfighters were all committed to NATO support operations through the Canadian Air Division in Europe. Of the six CF-104 squadrons, four squadrons were configured for nuclear strike and two squadrons were configured for tactical reconnaissance with VICON pods containing four 70-mm Vinten cameras.

Tactical reconnaissance tasks used the Vinten VICON under-fuselage camera pod. With deliveries to the CAF of CF-18 Hornets, the last CF-104s were retired from service on 28 February 1986.

Many CAF Starfighters were transferred to Turkey, which in early 1986 was allocated 20 for active operations, plus another 30 for spares. Turkey had lost around 110 CF-104/104Ds (from 239 received) in accidents to June 1983, or no less than 46 percent.

Canada acquired the following number of aircraft:

200	CF-104
38	CF-104D

Four West German Air Force F-104Gs in formation. Notice the emergency landing arresting hooks on the bottom of the aft fuselage. (MAP)

Denmark

The Royal Danish Air Force (RDAF) received a total of 40 F-104G Starfighters and 11 two-seat TF-104G/CF-104D trainers, mostly from Canada. An initial batch of 25 Canadair-built single- seat F-104Gs and four Lockheed TF-104Gs were supplied through the US Mutual Aid Program (MAP), the first being formally accepted on 29 June 1965. A second batch of 15 ex-RCAF CF-104s and seven CF-104Ds were bought from Canada in September 1971. Seven CF-104Ds were modified for the electronic countermeasures role.

Denmark acquired the following number of aircraft:

25	F-104G
15	(C)F-104G
7	CF-104D
4	TF-104G

West German Navy F-104Gs in formation. The German Navy had 100 F-104Gs in four squadrons. (MAP)

Federal Republic of Germany

West Germany was the largest user of the F-104, with a total of 915 F-104s. Germany took delivery of its first Starfighter, a Lockheed-built two-seat F-104F, at Norvenich to begin converting pilots in July 1960, and went on to order a total of 750 F/RF-104Gs, 30 F-104Fs and 136 two-seat TF-104Gs from Lockheed; 915 F-104s in all. In the mid-1970's, at their peak, these 915 F-104's equipped five heavy Luftwaffe fighter-bomber wings (nuclear-armed with standard NATO 1-MT store). Each wing comprised two squadrons with individual complements of 18 combat-ready aircraft, plus six in reserve and 10 in maintenance, or 52 Starfighters per wing.

Danish F-104G in olive drab paint landing in 1982. Notice the twin pylons on the fuselage. (MAP)

A Greek F-104G photographed with an unknown centerline store. The Royal Hellenic Air Force had 45 F-104Gs, with the first acquired in 1964. (MAP)

Completing this force were two interceptor wings, with another four F-104G squadrons, plus two tactical reconnaissance wings, with four RF-104G squadrons. From 1964 onwards, two naval attack wings replaced their Hawker Sea Hawks with 100 F-104Gs in four squadrons, each of 18 aircraft armed with AS-34 Kormoran anti-ship missiles. German forces lost about 270 Starfighters and 110 pilots in air and ground accidents, or just under 30 percent of their total force.

Franz J. Enzinger flew F-104Gs in the West German Air Force for over 1000 hours. When I asked how he liked flying the 104 he replied, "The F-104 was an enjoyable airplane to fly, easier to fly than the T-38 and was more responsive than the T-38."

When I asked him about the accident rates on the German F-104s he answered, "The accident numbers should consider the total number of F-104s flown. The WGAF had over 900 F-104s, the largest number of F-104s in any air force. There were several factors in the accidents. The F-104 J79 jet nozzles would fail open, resulting in no thrust. Initially there was no manual control to close the nozzle. Automatic pitch control on the G models caused a number of accidents. Insufficient parts resulted in cannibalization from other F-104s. More aircraft on the ground resulted in not enough aircraft flying to keep up pilot proficiency. Weather in Germany was also a factor, particularly compared to the weather in Arizona where most of the pilots trained."

An Italian F-104S carries two Sparrow air-to-air missiles. The F-104S is a third-generation Starfighter with an advanced weapons system and up-rated J79-GE-19 with 17,900 pounds thrust in afterburner. (Lockheed, Jim Fitzgerald collection)

Germany operated the last three F-104Gs and one two-seat TF-104G on avionics and systems development until the last German sortie on 22 May 1991.

Germany acquired the following number of aircraft:

30	F-104F
604	F-104G
145	RF-104G
136	TF-104G

Greece

Originally Greece was allocated 35 Canadair-built F-104Gs from 1961 MAP (Military Assistance Program) funding. HAF (Royal Hellenic Air Force) also received four TF-104Gs from Lockheed initial deliveries, plus another 10 MAP-funded Lockheed-built F-104Gs and six TF-104Gs from USAF stocks, to equip two squadrons each with 19 Starfighters for nuclear strike roles. The first HAF Starfighter unit began replacing its Republic F-84Fs in April 1964, and HAF's two F-104 squadrons then reverted to ground-attack with conventional weapons in the early 1970s.

Italy

Fiat produced 200 F-104Gs for Italy, Germany and the Netherlands, including 125 for the Italian Air Force, which received a prototype from the US in March 1962, followed by the initial flight of the first F-104G from Turin on 9 June 1962 to re-equip three F-86K Sabre all-weather interceptor squadrons. The 20 RF-104Gs were equipped with the Orpheus reconnaissance pod. F-104Gs and TF-104Gs first entered service in 1963. The Italian Air Force's last F-104G fighter-bomber unit replaced its Starfighters with Tornados in early 1983, leaving one squadron as the last combat operator of earlier-generation Starfighters with Orpheus sensor pod equipped RF-104Gs. The two-seaters remained in service in 1995, in limited numbers.

The first two F-104S aircraft, armed with two AIM-7 Sparrow 3 and four AIM-9 sidewinder Air to Air Missiles, were converted by Lockheed from AMI F-104Gs at Palmdale, their flight tests starting in December 1966. The first production F-104S was delivered on 9 June 1969.

The Italian Air Force was still flying the F-104S with a number of upgrades in 2003 — last Air Force operational Starfighters.

Italy acquired the following number of aircraft:

113	F-104G
12	RF-104G
24	TF-104G
1	F-104S prototype
205	F-104S

Japan

In 1960 the F-104J was selected to replace the JASDF's F-86F Sabres in a $207 million joint US/Japanese program with local manufacture by Mitsubishi and Ishikawajima/Harima, the latter group producing the J79-IHI-1 1A powerplants. Initial orders comprised 180 F-104J fighter-bombers plus 20 locally-assembled two-seat F-104DJ trainers, with deliveries starting from Lockheed in early 1962. A further 30 F-104Js were then ordered for local production, with deliveries by 1967. This program was completed in January 1965, with seven squadrons re-equipped. Mitsubishi assembled or built a total of 210 F-104J Starfighters at Komaki between 1 April 1962 and 2 December 1967. The first example, built by Lockheed Burbank, was first flown on July 1961, before being shipped to Japan and reassembled to fly at Komaki on 8 March 1962. The second and third examples followed a similar pattern with 17 more F-104Js, assembled by Mitsubishi from knocked-down kits, before Japanese production began to equip seven all-weather interceptor squadrons between October 1962 and December 1967. Mitsubishi also assembled another 20 two-seat F-104DJ trainers

Four Japan Air Self Defense Force F-104Js. Three of the F-104Js have fuselage-mounted Sidewinder launch rails. (Lockheed, Dave Steinbacher collection)

Japan ASDF F-104Js peel off from their formation flight. Notice the sidewinder rails on the wing and fuselage. (Lockheed, Dave Steinbacher collection)

Jordanian Air Force F-104A in 1995, one of 36 in the Jordanian Air Force. (MAP)

from Lockheed-built kits between 1962 and 1964.

Japan acquired the following number of aircraft:

210 F-104J
20 F-104DJ

Jordan

A total of 36 early ex-USAF Starfighters were promised to Jordan by the US government in April 1966, and an initial batch of three F-104As and three two-seat F-104Bs were airlifted to the Royal Jordanian Air Force in early 1967. Apart from one F-104A, which had already crashed, they were almost immediately withdrawn to Turkey at the outbreak of the six-day Middle East war between 5-10 June 1967. A large part of the Arab air forces, including most of the RJAF's operational strength, was destroyed on the ground by initial Israeli air attacks. It was not until late 1968 that RJAF pilots and ground crews resumed Starfighter training in the United States.

The first six of 18 ex-USAF F-104As and four F-104Bs, were initially flown by Pakistan air force pilots before their receipt by Jordan in mid-1969. A visit to Washington by King Hussein earlier in 1969 had resulted in President Nixon agreeing to supply Jordan with a second squadron of 18 F-104As. The 18 were to be transferred from Taiwan's Nationalist Chinese air force storage following their replacement by F-104Gs, after the Jordanian monarch had pointed out that he had been offered MiG-21s by the USSR for about one-third the price of comparable Western equipment. Number 9 Squadron was sent with its F104As to Pakistan to help out in the 1971 war with India, in which it is believed to have suffered several losses. The RJAF was reported to

Netherlands F-104G(R) taxiing in 1982 with the Oldelft Orpheus reconnaissance pod. The Orpheus pod carried five cameras and an infrared scanner. (MAP)

have operated about 20 F-104As and four "B"s in two squadrons by July 1979, to be replaced by 34 Mirage F1s.

Jordan acquired the following number of aircraft:

36 F-104A
6 F-104B

A Norwegian F-104G in 1977 with four external fuel tanks and an unknown centerline store. (MAP)

Netherlands

Most Dutch tactical units committed to NATO re-equipped from Republic F-84F/RF-84s and Lockheed RT-33As with F/RF-104Gs ordered for the Royal Netherlands Air Force. A total of 138 F-104s were ordered. All RF-104Gs were equipped with Orpheus sensor pods containing five TA-8M cameras and an infra-red line-scanner for tactical reconnaissance.

The Starfighters entered service with the RNAF in December 1962 and were operated until November 1984, when they were replaced with European built General Dynamics F-16A and F-16Bs.

The Netherlands acquired the following number of aircraft:

95 F-104G
25 RF0194G
18 TF-104G

Four F-104Gs of the Spanish Air Force. Spain had 21 F-104s and operated them for seven years with no accidents. (Lockheed, Dave Steinbacher collection)

Norway

Royal Norwegian Air Force (RNoAF) received the first of its Starfighters in 1963: 16 Lockheed-built RF-104Gs for reconnaissance, three Canadair-built F-104Gs, and two Lockheed TF-104G trainers. These were later supplemented by two ex-Luftwaffe TF-104Gs from Luke AFB in the US.

In May 1973, RnoAF further acquired18 surplus CAF CF-104s and four CF-104Ds from storage at Prestwick, including overhaul and modification, to equip a second squadron for anti-ship roles with Martin Bullpup Anti-Ship Missiles. The last of the Norwegian Starfighters were phased out in early 1983. Only six of 45 Starfighters (13.3 percent) were lost in Norwegian service in over 56,000 flying hours.

Norway acquired the following number of aircraft:

3 F-104G
16 RF-104G
18 (C)F-104G
4 TF-104G
4 CF-104D

A Norwegian two-place TF-104G in 1978, one of four TF models in the Royal Norwegian Air Force. (MAP)

Pakistan

Ten F-104As and two F-104Bs were initially delivered through MAP from the USAF from 15 September 1961 onwards. Two F-104As were later delivered from Taiwan as combat attrition replacements for 1965 losses during the war with India. In 1971 Pakistan received 10 F-104As on loan from Jordan. These 10 were returned to Jordan in 1972 when Pakistan phased out its last four Starfighters.

Pakistan acquired the following number of aircraft:

14 F-104A
2 F-104B

Spain

Eighteen Canadair-built F-104Gs and three Lockheed built TF-104Gs were delivered through MAP to Spain, the first arriving on 5 March 1965. These replaced the North American F-86F Sabres. Spain was unique in operating its small number of Starfighters without a single accident during their seven years of service and 17,500 flying hours. For-

Turkish F-104S ASA in 1991, one of 40 Turkish 'S' models. Italy and Turkey were the only Air Forces to have the third generation 'S' models. (MAP)

mal retirement of the Starfighters was on 31 May 1972.

Spain acquired the following number of aircraft:

18 F-104G
3 TF-104G

Taiwan

Information on the actual quantities of F-104s in the Chinese Nationalist Air Force is sketchy. Initial F-104s were received in 1960. Over the years Taiwan obtained F-104As, F-104Bs, F-104Gs (starting in 1964), TF-104Gs, RF-104Gs, F-104Ds, F-104Js and F-104DJs (1987).

Early-model F-104As, F-104Bs, and F-104Ds were withdrawn from service in the early 1980s. In 1990, the RoCAF's (Republic of China Air Force) remaining Starfighters equipped one reconnaissance and six tactical fighter squadrons, and some were scheduled to continue in service until 1996. Their armament package included AIM-9J Sidewinder Air-Air-Missiles and locally developed Sky Sword I and II Infra Red and semi-active radar homing AAMs. Total F-104s in the Republic of China Air Force since 1960 is estimated at 219 Starfighters.

Turkey

Turkey obtained its first 36 F-104Gs and four TF-104Gs in 1965 to 1966. These aircraft took part in the 1976 invasion of Cypress. Through the years, Turkey obtained more F-104Gs, CF-104s, RF-104Gs, and F-104S models. Many of these Starfighters came from NATO countries that were phasing out the 104s, such as Belgium, Germany, Netherlands, and Canada. Forty of the later-model F-104S Starfighters were bought new from Italy starting in December 1974 and were armed with Selenia-built Sparrow Air-to-Air Missiles.

In all, Turkey appears to have received just over 400 Starfighters, although many of these have been withdrawn from service or cannibalized for spares. Large numbers have also been lost in crashes, and although no overall accident statistics are available, only 21 of the original 40 F-104S interceptors bought from Italy were still in service by late 1987.

A Turkish two-place F-104D in 1987. (MAP)

LARGEST VENTURE

While the United States Air Force only ordered 296 F-104s, the worldwide manufacture and use brought the total 104s built to 2,578, making it the largest international co-operative venture in the history of the aerospace business.

MODIFICATIONS

7

TO THE EDGE OF SPACE

A number of modifications were made for one-of-a-kind or small numbers of Lockheed F-104s. The following are some of the particularly interesting modifications to the basic F-104 models.

JF-104 RCS TEST AIRCRAFT

A single YF-104A, s/n 55-2961 was modified in the late 1950s by NASA to pick up the reaction control system (RCS) testing that had been started on the Bell X-1B. The Bell X-1B rocket plane developed cracks in its main fuel tank, resulting in a permanent grounding of the research rocket plane. The data and experience from these tests were needed to support the X-15 program. The F-104 had very similar performance to the X-1B, and made a logical substitute aircraft.

Modifications included installing the hydrogen peroxide powered reaction control system from the Bell X-1B on the F-104. Roll control was installed in pods on the wing tips, which housed the reaction control motor and a hydrogen peroxide tank. For pitch and yaw control, four reaction control motors in a cruciform layout were installed in the nose, with the hydrogen peroxide in a tank just forward of the cockpit. The reaction controller in the cockpit had proportional control, varying output with the deflection of the handle.

A total of 28 flights were flown with the control system between 1959 and 1961. The maximum altitude attained during these flights was 83,000 feet. A number of improvements in cockpit attitude display information resulted from these tests.

NF-104A AEROSPACE TRAINER

Three F-104As serials 56-756, 56-760, and 56-762 were modified by Lockheed as Aerospace Trainers for the United States Air Force. The Aerospace Trainer was to gain pilot experience in space flight in the areas of boost to sub-orbit, zero gravity operation, reaction control system use, and reentry maneuvering.

Major modifications included adding a rocket engine in the tail of the 104, extending the wings two feet each, installing a reaction flight control system and modifying the inlet system.

In addition to the standard J79 engine, a 6,000-pound thrust Rocketdyne AR2-3 rocket engine was added in the tail of the NF-104A. This rocket engine used the same JP-4 fuel as the F-104s J79 engine plus hydrogen peroxide as an oxidizer. The hydrogen peroxide was carried in two tanks replacing the F-104 auxiliary fuel cell.

The reaction control system was required because of the high altitudes that the NF-104A would reach. In the thin air above 90,000 feet, normal flight control surfaces are completely ineffective. The reaction control system uses tiny rocket motors mounted in the nose and wing tips that fire individually to replace the inputs that are normally provided by the ailerons, elevator, and rudder. A separate control handle in the cockpit fired the tiny rocket motors in the appropriate axis (pitch, roll and yaw) to fly the aircraft.

For safety redundancy there were 12 of these tiny rocket motors: two motors in each wing tip with

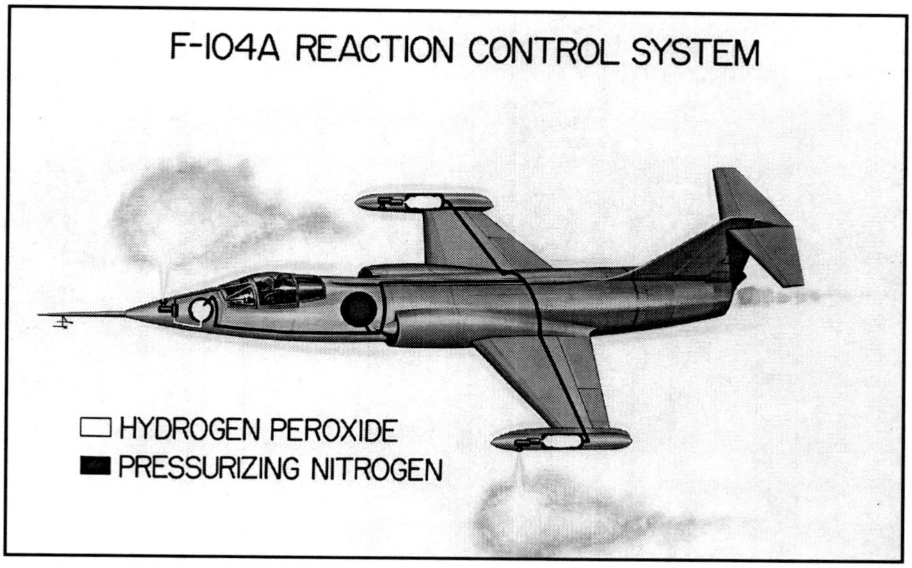

JF-104 reaction flight control system test bed details, showing locations of the reaction control system. Tanks in the nose and wing tips hold hydrogen peroxide with the nitrogen tank aft of the cockpit. (NASA Dryden via Tony Landis)

Cockpit of the JF-104 on 4 August 1959. Notice the separate control stick for the reaction controls in the upper left side of the cockpit. (NASA Dryden via Tony Landis)

one on top and one on the bottom were for roll control. In the nose were two motors on the top and two on the bottom for pitch control and two each on the left and right side of the nose for yaw control.

The F-104's wing span was increased by four feet with two wing-tip extensions. This increased the total wing area to provide additional lift.

The inlet cone was redesigned for the higher Mach numbers of the NF-104A. The cone was 20 inches

The JF-104 reaction flight control system test bed. The NASA JF-104 #961 (818), equipped with reaction flight controls, is shown here on the lakebed at Edwards AFB on 4 August 1959. The wing-tip pods house the roll reaction control rocket motors and the hydrogen peroxide tanks. (NASA Dryden via Tony Landis)

longer than the standard cone, and the extension was at a different angle from the original cone. Intake air had to be slowed to subsonic speed before entering the engine. The original cone design optimized engine performance up to Mach 2, but the NF-104 mission plan called for Mach 2.2 speeds.

Zoom Maneuvers

To reach the high altitudes above 100,000 feet, a zoom maneuver was used. While standard F-104s used the zoom maneuver to reach high altitudes, the NF-104A reached even higher altitudes with the 6000 pounds additional thrust from the rocket motor, and had the capability to control the aircraft with the reaction controls in the thin atmosphere. The NF-104A reached an altitude 118,860 feet in an unofficial record flight by USAF Major Robert Smith on 6 December 1963.

A typical NF-104A zoom climb maneuver started acceleration at about 35,000 feet altitude and went into a 3.5G pull-up at Mach 2.15. The J79 engine would be shut down going through 70,000 to 80,000 feet when the engine reached its temperature limit. The pilot controlled the pitch attitude with the Reaction Control System, dampers being turned on going through 90,000 feet. After the rocket engine shut down, the aircraft coasted over the top of the trajectory to maximum altitude, and then descent started with the speed brakes extended. J79 engine restart was usually attempted below 75,000 feet with successful starts as high as 75,000 feet.

Flight Testing

Flight testing of the NF-104A had two steps. Category I contractor testing at Lockheed involved 50 flights and started 9 July 1963. The first NF-104A was delivered to the United States Air Force Flight Test Center on 1 October 1963 for Category II USAF testing at Edwards Air Force Base. A total of 68 flights were flown. Once this was complete in 1965, the NF-104s went to the Aerospace Research Pilots School. (Later the name changed to the United States Air Force Test Pilot School).

Problems - NF-104 History

Several problems occurred during the flights of the NF-104A. During a record altitude attempt by (then) Colonel Chuck Yeager, on 10 December 1963, at 101,000 feet Yeager could not lower the nose from the near vertical climb with the reaction controls. The aircraft departed into an oscillating spin, and, after tumbling over the top of the trajectory at 104,000 feet, ended up in a spin direction reversal at 65,000 into a stabilized flat spin. With little airflow to the engine to restart it there was no hydraulics to power the normal flight controls. Yeager finally had to eject at 11,000 feet. Subsequently, a new recovery system was installed

Roll control rocket motors are fired in a ground test of the reaction control system on 1 October 1959 on the JF-104. (NASA Dryden via Tony Landis)

Firing the yaw control of the reaction flight control system on the JF-104 during a test on 6 January 1960. Both the pitch and yaw control rocket motors are in the nose. (NASA Dryden via Tony Landis)

Early checkout run of the 6,000-pound thrust Rocketdyne AR2-3 rocket engine on NF-104A S/N 762. Notice the fire truck. JP-4 fuel was used in the rocket engine along with a Hydrogen Peroxide oxidizer. (Lockheed, Jim Fitzgerald collection)

on the remaining two NF-104As using a drogue fired anti-spin chute.

The two NF-104s continued to fly until December 1971. In the Aerospace Research Pilots School approximately 50 pilots flew the NF-104s on 302 flights. Many graduates from the school were ultimately selected to become astronauts.

Over time, there were several incidents involving hydrogen peroxide and damage to the aircraft. Some of them occurred on the ground, caused by sump oxidation and leaks that resulted in explosions. Fixes were incorporated and flying continued. In one in-flight case in 1971, there was a large explosion after attempting to light the rocket engine, followed by a second explosion that blew the rocket engine and a portion of the rudder off. The NF-104A made a successful emergency landing on the dry lakebed at EAFB. Cause was traced to high-pressure hydrogen peroxide leaks.

The Aerospace Trainer program was shut down in December 1971 with the Air Force's diminishing need for training space pilots after the cancellation of the X-20 Dyna-Soar and the Manned Orbiting Laboratory (MOL) programs.

F-104 Space Capsule? CL-361

Some publications have printed photos and drawings showing a mockup and artist's drawing (left on page 87) with a caption stating there was a plan to develop the nose and cockpit of the F-104 as a space capsule for astronaut training. A rocket plume is visible in the artist's drawing and a rocket nozzle is visible on the back of the mockup. A caption for the mockup said the program only went as far as the mockup stage.

The photo at the right top of page 87 shows the program went a lot further than the wood mockup stage. The metal assemblies of portions of three "capsules" are visible. What appears to be an F-104 fuselage section is behind the cockpit section.

The Lockheed design number for this program was CL-361. One

Two NF-104s parked at the Test Pilot school at Edwards Air Force Base. (AFFTC History Office via Tony Landis)

Space Capsule? This artwork depicts a purported high-altitude space capsule for training astronauts using the front end of the F-104. (Lockheed via Phil Sullivan)

This photo obtained by the author shows actual hardware for the "space capsule." There are parts including fins for three vehicles in the photo. (Lockheed, Jim Upton collection)

reference in a list of CL numbers by a Lockheed design engineer said there were no records on this model, indicating the program was probably classified and the reports were probably destroyed.

The True Story

Several people who worked on the program gave me the true story. Phil Sullivan was the original program manager on the project, and Mel Cassidy and John Peterson were Lockheed Aerodynamics Engineers on the program.

First, this was not a space capsule for astronaut training. It was development work for a new ejection system for high-speed aircraft with capability to over Mach 4, and high altitudes, called the Mach 4 Ejectable Escape Capsule. The concept was to use a capsule to protect the crew, and use a parachute to bring the crew down while protected by the cockpit section.

The hardware shown on these pages is for the sled tests that were run at the Edwards Air Force Base Ejection track test facility. Three test vehicles were built.

F-104 Escape Capsule

Three capsules were built for sled tests that were run at Edwards Air Force Base. Some capsules were used multiple times. The purpose was to develop a high-speed escape system that could be used on an F-104 or other aircraft. Tests were run from zero speed to Mach 1.4. The nose capsule reached heights above launch varying from 100 feet at zero speed, to over 1000 feet at Mach 1.4. The capsule and triangular cross section stabilizing fins added lift to the rocket-powered capsule.

The sled propulsion system included an F-104 shaped section that mated to the F-104 nose capsule. The Mach 1.2 test was completely successful with good stability in flight, correct sequencing of all the initiator functions, and protection of the pilot (The Mach 1.4 test sled left the track due to an incorrectly installed bolt.).

The testing validated the concept of capsule escape systems, but there was too much weight and volume in the large stabilizing fins for the small F-104. An improved design to the rocket ejection seats was able to meet the need of the Starfighter.

Three completed escape capsules ready for testing. (Lockheed via Pete Clukey)

In truth, the "space capsule" turned out to be an ejection escape capsule test vehicle that used the front end of the F-104. One of three capsules built for the test program hangs from a crane in building 360 at Lockheed Burbank. (Lockheed via Pete Clukey)

Photos of the actual sled shot at Edwards AFB of the "ejection capsule," showing a sequence of four photo frames from the high-speed movie camera. Frame 1; Capsule leaving the sled track with rocket plume visible. Frame 2; Rocket burnout with capsule still climbing; Frame 3. Drogue chute pulls parachute out. Frame 4; Capsule recovery chute inflates. (Lockheed via Pete Clukey)

Mockup of the CL-361 at Lockheed's Building 360 in Burbank. Several publications have shown this photo with a caption stating this was a design for a space capsule for training astronauts using F-104 parts. (Lockheed via Pete Clukey)

ZELL – NO RUNWAY

In June 1966 Lockheed announced the successful launch of the 1500-mile-an-hour F-104 without the use of a runway. This occurred in 1963 in a secret test program at Edwards AFB. Lockheed was under a contract from the West German Air Force. The test was to demonstrate the fighter's capability to carry out combat operations without the use of runways for take-off.

The ZELL (ZEro Length Launch) program was to demonstrate the technique that would enable the F-104 to take off from small clearings or sheltered areas. Lockheed test pilot Ed Brown flew the flights. Subsequent tests and demonstrations were made in Germany at Letchfield base

ZELL (ZEro Length Launch) F-104 leaps into the air as black smoke covers the launch ramp. The ZELL system uses a 120,000-pound thrust rocket to boost the F-104 to flying speed, at which point the rocket booster is jettisoned. (Lockheed, Dave Steinbacher collection)

near Munich in May 1966 using two F-104Gs. The Luftwaffe investigated the Zero Length Launch system as a means of dispersing their Starfighters around the country. In time of tension the concept envisioned fleets of nuclear-armed F-104Gs being trucked out to the countryside and launched if required.

The Zell configuration used a North American Aviation Rocketdyne solid rocket mounted under the rear fuselage that developed 120,000 pounds of thrust. The rocket was originally designed for the Martin TM-61 Matador nuclear cruise missile in the 1950s. An adjustable

A long climb to the cockpit. Loading Lockheed test pilot Ed Brown in the cockpit of the ZELL F-104G before a rocket launch take-off. (Lockheed, Jim Fitzgerald collection)

Close-up of the ZELL launch ramp. The rocket used was a North American Rocketdyne solid rocket originally designed for the Martin TM-61 Matador cruise missile in the 1950s. The rocket developed 120,000 pounds of thrust. (Lockheed, Jim Upton Collection)

Rocket and launcher on F-104 #749 with an ALSOR (Air Launched SOunding Rocket) on 16 February 1961. The 253-pound rocket produced a thrust of 5,395 pounds and reached an altitude of 383,000 feet after launch from the F-104. (NASA Dryden via Tony Landis)

ramp was used that would elevate the ZELL to the correct angle for launch. Rocket booster would be jettisoned after launch. The program never went beyond the demonstration phase.

F-104 Rocket Launcher

An F-104A modification culminated in launching research rockets to altitudes as high as 383,000 feet. The F-104 was used as the recoverable first stage of a two-stage aircraft rocket combination. Advantages of this combination were a highly flexible launch site that could be located anywhere within the aircraft's range, and the F-104 provided a means of controlling flight parameters at second-stage ignition. The air launches were estimated to cost one-third the cost of ground launched rockets.

NASA needed atmospheric-density information at altitudes between 100,000 feet and 500,000 feet in support of the X-15 program. These altitudes are above the reach of weather balloons (100,000 feet), and below minimum satellite orbits.

Lockheed had made modifications to F-104A s/n 60749 for a series of air-launch tests in an earlier prototype weapons-systems program. Modification entailed provisions for a

An ALSOR rocket on the F-104 with hydraulically actuated trapeze extended before launch. The upper part of the rack and trapeze were from the MB-1 program, an earlier classified weapons system program on the F-104. (NASA Dryden via Tony Landis)

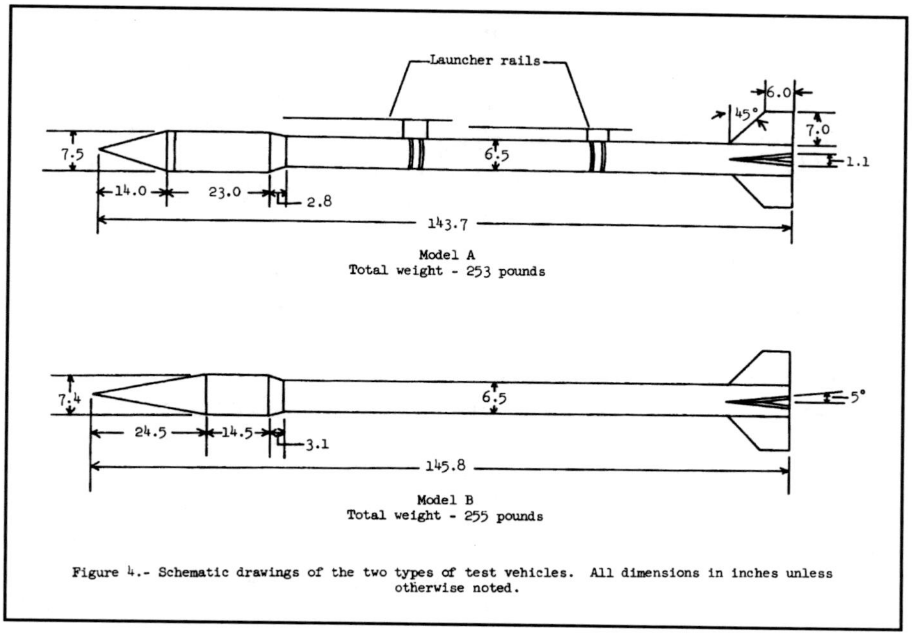

Viper rockets Model 'A' and 'B' details. Model 'A' weighed 253 pounds and was 143.7 inches long. Model 'B' rocket weighed 255 pounds and was 145.8 inches long. Model 'A' rocket had a little larger space in the nose for the payload and was designed to reach altitudes of 800,000 feet. (NASA)

hydraulically actuated MB-1 launcher rack which, when retracted, is almost flush with the fuselage of the aircraft. A modified Sidewinder launcher rack was attached to the MB-1 rack.

In flight, the rack extended five feet below the F-104. The separation and angle were sufficient to prevent rocket exhaust from entering the aircraft engine inlet.

Five Viper rockets were launched in this program as the second stage vehicle. Two rocket configurations were used. Rocket motors produced 5,395 pounds of thrust for the 145-inch long 255-pound rocket. The nose section carried an inflatable Mylar sphere that was ejected at the trajectory peak. The metallic sphere was tracked by ground radar, which provided upper atmosphere density and wind velocity data.

Launch was accomplished during a vertical climb at speeds from .76 Mach number to 1.4 Mach number. Second-stage launch altitude occurred from 28, 600 feet to 51,000 feet. Highest payload altitude reached was 383,000 feet.

These tests validated the practicality of the method employed to utilize the energy of an aircraft like the 104 as a first-stage booster and launcher for sounding rockets.

New Land Speed Record?

A highly modified former F-104A Starfighter (Lockheed s/n 1076, USAF s/n 56-763) called the North American Eagle is now a racecar that will make a land speed record attempt. The current land speed record is 763 mph held by RAF pilot Andy Green.

The "North American Eagle" is built from an F-104A fuselage and has a General Electric J79-15 engine that produces 18,500 pounds thrust. The engine is a later model than what originally flew in the F-104A and came from a McDonnell F-4.

Project Manager Ed Shadle is the owner and driver. Partner and co-owner is Keith Zanghi. The "North American Eagle" will be tested up to speeds of 300 mph using rubber tires, and then 300 mph and higher speeds will be run with wheels machined from solid blocks of aluminum which are good up to 900 mph. Rubber tires do not hold up well above 400 mph.

F-104A Lockheed msn 1076, USAF s/n 56-763 landing at Edwards Air Force Base after an X-15 chase flight on 8 July 1964. This Starfighter is now being converted to a racecar for an attempt at a new land speed record. (NASA Dryden)

Monoculars in the F-104 were part of a 1960s NASA investigation into approach and landing visibility for use in low L/D aircraft (like lifting bodies and the National Aero Space Plane). Two wide-angle overlapping periscopes provided the pilot in the rear seat of the F-104B with a stereoscopic view. (NASA Drydenvia Tony Landis)

Speed tests will be in a build-up fashion with different locations used for the higher speeds. Current plans include low speed runs under 300 mph in the latter part of 2003 at Moses Lake Washington, which has a 13,000-foot runway. Additional low speed runs may be run at El Mirage dry lake in California. Bonneville Salt flats in Utah could be used for up to 500 mph. Bonneville is too short for speeds higher than 500 mph, and Black Rock Desert in Nevada is one of the candidates for higher speeds. Another candidate is Cold Lake Alberta, where the lower temperatures would result in the speed of sound occurring at speeds closer to 600 mph, allowing transsonic problems to be worked out at a lower speed.

Current distance estimate for just acceleration to 800 mph is three-and-a-half miles. A total distance of 11 miles is needed for the record run. Braking is accomplished using five systems. Initial braking at the end of the speed run is done with the standard F-104 speed brakes on the aft fuselage and a small drogue chute. When the car is slowed to 300 mph, the main drag chute is deployed which slows the car to 125 to 150 mph where the disk brakes can be applied. If these systems fail, the driver can steer the car into an aircraft carrier catch net that has been tested to 300 mph. Shadle estimates the completion date for this project to be in 2004.

Notable Modifications

The outstanding modifications to the 104 were the NF-104A Aerospace Trainer, which reached an altitude of 118,860 feet with its added rocket in the tail, and the ZELL F-104 with its capability to take off loaded with weapons without using a runway.

Is this an F-104? After a nose radome change during some radar tests, F-104 s/n 60790 has a completely different look. The radome was borrowed from a Lockheed U-2. Notice the relocation of the pitot-static tube to the bottom of the fuselage, replacing the standard long pitot-static probe on the nose. (Lockheed, Jim Fitzgerald collection)

8 Civilian F-104s

NASA Through Air Shows

There are only three civilian-registered, flyable Lockheed F-104s today. Two are in Florida and one is in Arizona. Over the years there has been a number of civilian registered F-104s in the United States. This started with the "House Aircraft" that Lockheed-California Company owned and used as a sales tool demonstrator of the F-104 combat capabilities.

Lockheed's N104L

Two-place TF-104 s/n 5702, registered N104L, (and later N90500) was basically similar to the TF-104G procured by the United States Air Force for foreign air forces under the Military Assistance Program (MAP). The TF-104G was a specialized, multi-purpose fighter-trainer that performed most F-104G missions with nearly equal competence and fulfilled all training requirements for the F-104G. The two-place F-104 is not merely a trainer — it is a fighting piece of equipment as well.

Lockheed test pilots flew the demonstration flights. Depending on the observers' interests, a particular type of mission was flown. Examples were a NASARR Air-To-Air demonstration, an Inertial Navigator /Tacan /NASSAR demonstration, a Maximum Range Bombing Mission, and a Low Altitude Penetration mission. Many of these flights were flown out of Lockheed's Palmdale facility in the Mojave Desert, but they could be set up for other locations as well. When Lockheed was done with N104L it was sold to the Netherlands Air Force.

NASA F-104s

Through the years, NASA Dryden at Edwards Air Force Base in California used a variety of chase and support aircraft. First acquired in August 1956, Lockheed F-104s were the most versatile work horses in Dryden's stable of research and support aircraft, with 11 of them flying mostly research missions over 39 years. A good example of the type of tasks performed is on the X-15 program. A modified F-104 tested the reaction control system for the X-15. The F-104's short wings and low lift to drag ratio made it ideal to simulate the X-15 landing profile, which the F-104s often undertook before X-15 flights. This was used for pilot profi-

Lockheed's two-place TF-104G Starfighter registered N104L was the first civil registered F-104. Labeled as the "Free World Defender," it was owned by Lockheed California Company and assigned to demonstration flights for military guests. (Lockheed, Dave Steinbacher collection)

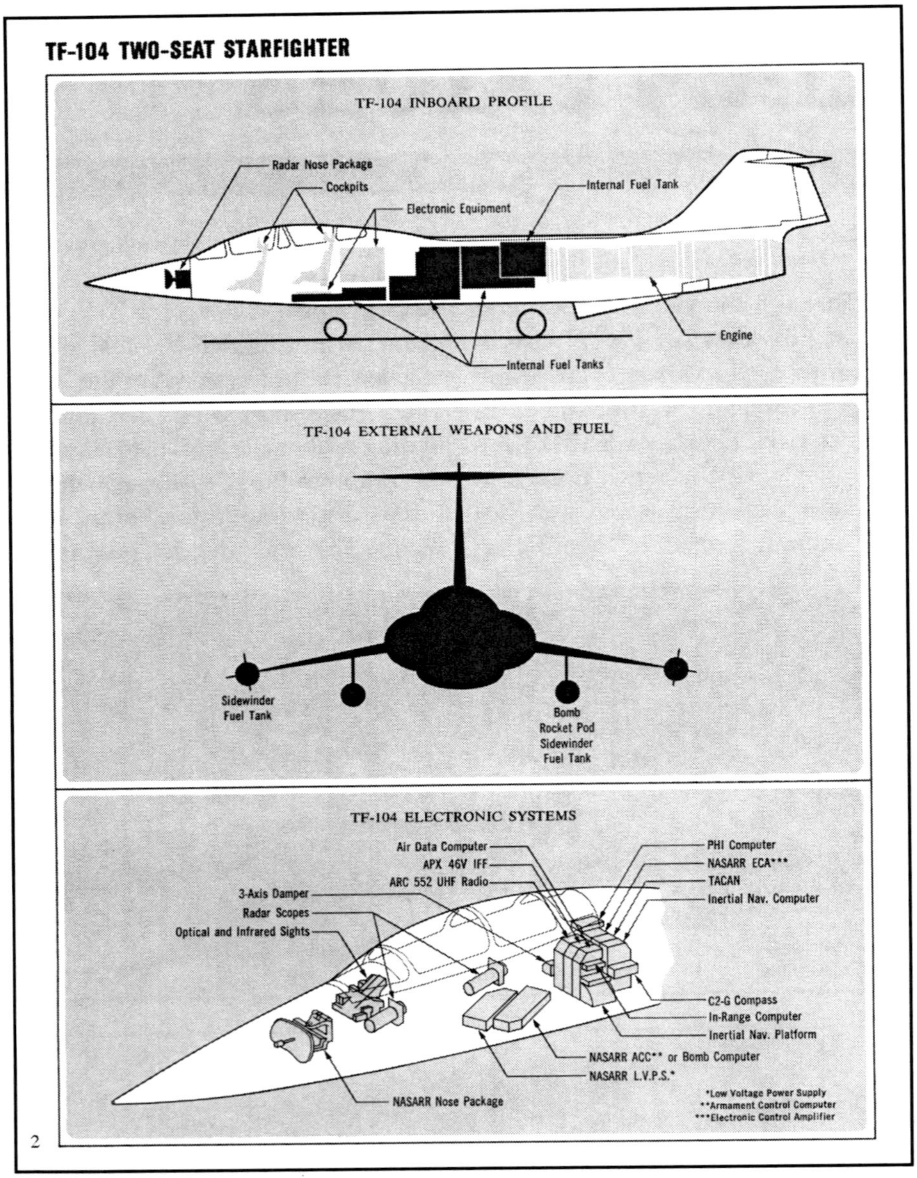

Inboard profile of the Lockheed TF-104G, showing the locations of main components. Location of the internal avionics is shown in the bottom diagram. (Lockheed via Tom Laughlin)

ciency. The 104s were also used as chase aircraft on the X-15 program.

NASA's initial group of four Starfighters (a YF-104A, two F-104As and a two seat F-104B) arrived between August 1956 and December 1959. To support X-15 activities, three special F-104Ns went to NASA in 1963. As the initial F-104 fleet aged, a pair of two-seat TF-104Gs and a single-seat F-104G joined the Dryden inventory in June 1975. Between 1975 and 1990 the older F-104s were retired. As the F-104s phased out, the F-18s began arriving in 1984. F-104 N826NA made its 1,415th and last flight on 3 February 1994. The last two TF-104s were retired in September 1995, ending a 39-year involvement with the aircraft by NASA.

It is interesting to note that you would see the NASA 104s with "U.S. AIR FORCE" markings and the USAF star and bar emblem along with "NASA" markings. In many cases, Air Force serial numbers were still on the aircraft. In later years the

NASA 811 flying a chase flight on the Martin Marietta X-24B, a research vehicle modified by the Air Force Flight Dynamics Laboratory to explore aerodynamic configurations. It was also used for testing precision landing techniques for the Space Shuttle. (NASA Dryden via Tony Landis)

NASA 104s were painted in a civilian-type paint scheme, typically blue and white, and carried a civilian 'N' number registration.

Svetkoff's Starfighters, Inc.

Based in Clearwater, Florida, Svetkoff's Starfighters, Inc. is billed as the fastest show on earth. Currently flying two F-104s in air shows across the United States and Canada, this formation jet demonstration team has turned out to be a real crowd pleaser.

Their aircraft collection consists of a single-seat Canadian CF-104 and a two-place CF-104D, formerly flown by the Norwegian air force. Pilots Rick "Comrade" Svetkoff and Tom "Sharkbait" Delashaw perform a series of high-speed passes, rolls and pull-ups showcasing the aircraft's speed and unmatched rate of climb. Keeping the aircraft within show boundaries at the high speeds means six to seven 'G' turns. The aircraft nearly reach supersonic speed during the fast passes and only drop below 350 knots for photo passes and landing.

The unique howling sound of the F-104 engine can be controlled and produced on demand both during taxi and in the air. This sound is unique to F-104's with the GE-J79-3, –7 or –11 engines. It results from the configuration of the primary and secondary exhaust nozzles on the tailpipe (see diagram on page 28). Exhaust gases rushing past the gap between the primary nozzle and the secondary nozzle, which is larger in diameter and aft of the primary, produce the howl the same way blowing across the opening of a bottle produces a distinctive sound. Moving the throttle to a specific engine rpm range creates the howl on demand.

In landing after a typical 17-minute show, one aircraft lands using

Five NASA F-104s in formation flight on 11 April 1975: F-104N #811- Bill Dana; F-104N #812- Tom McMurtry; F-104A #818-Einar Enevoldson; F-104A #820 Gary Krier; F-104B #819-Fitz Fulton and Ray Young. The photo was taken from T-38 #821, with Don Mallick and Bob Rhine. (NASA Dryden via Tony Landis)

NASA F-104N 812 flying chase with NASA's Lockheed YF-12 Blackbird. (NASA Dryden via Tony Landis)

NASA 826 was a former WGAF F-104G, shown here while landing at EAFB. (NASA Dryden via Tony Landis)

Remote External Viewing Display (REVD) lens on F-104 NASA 825. This lens system was tested as part of the X-30/NASP (National Aero Space Plane) program. This was a continuation of the investigation of approach and landing visibility started in the 1960s with the Monocular system on the F-104. (NASA Dryden via Tony Landis)

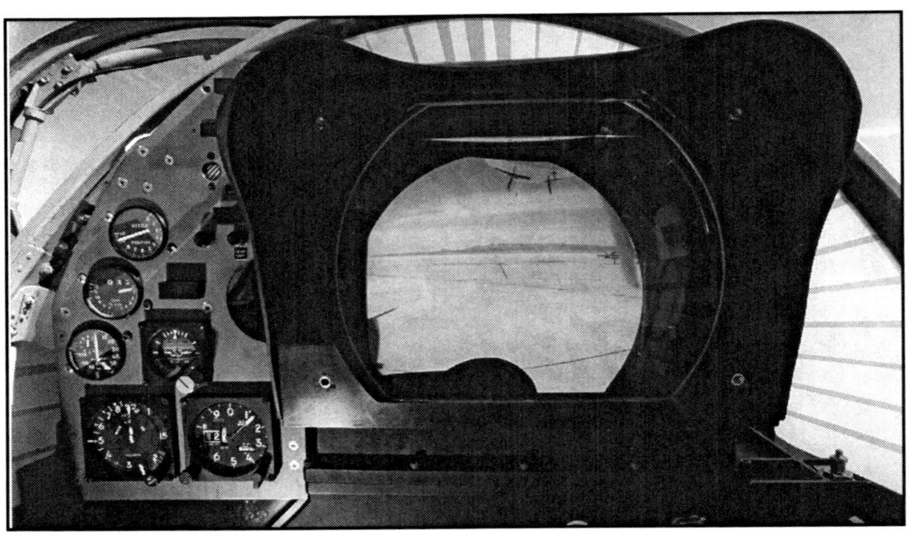

A view of the rear cockpit of NASA 825, showing the Remote External Viewing Display viewer. (NASA Dryden via Tony Landis)

a drag chute, creating an interesting visual for the crowds, while the other 104 lands using aerodynamic braking by holding a nose high attitude after main gear touchdown.

This formation jet demonstration team is currently flying 12 to 16 shows per year with their F-104s. This is in addition to occasional contract work flying supersonic chase or training space flight candidates for Space Adventures.

Space Adventures

In 2002, Space Adventures, Ltd., the company responsible for the first two space tourist flights to

NASA 826 takes off on its last flight before being retired on 3 February 1994. N826NA flew 1,415 flights at NASA before retiring. (NASA via Tony Landis)

the International Space Station, partnered with Starfighters, Inc., the world's fastest air show team, to utilize the F-104s, the original astronaut trainer, to conduct space flight training and orientation.

This F-104 program provides space flight participants first-hand experience with the unique characteristics of high performance vehicles; high speed, excess thrust, high-'g', and high-altitude flight, similar to many phases of sub-orbital and orbital space flight.

Space Adventures has been offering similar space flight training from Zhukovsky Air Base in Russia since 1998, using the MiG-25 "Foxbat," the world's fastest combat aircraft, sending over 500 clients to "edge-of-space" altitudes exceeding 85,000 feet.

Mark Sherman's F-104

Mark Sherman, President of the Classic Jet Aircraft Association, owns and flies a CF-104D based at Williams-Gateway airport near Phoenix, Arizona. Mark Sherman flew A-7s in the Navy and has had a fascination for the F-104 Starfighter from the time he would go to watch them flying out of Luke Air Force Base during his college years. Years later, when an F-104 was advertised in 'Trade-A-Plane', he ended up buying it. The aircraft was originally owned by Jim Robertson, who founded the Combat Jets flying museum in Houston, Texas. From there it went to the Experimental Aircraft Association Museum in Wisconsin, and Sherman obtained it in 1996.

His primary flights are for pleasure; business; some air shows; research and development government contracts; and for fuel, oil additive evaluations. He says owning and operating an F-104 is not a sideline project, it is a way of life. Because of the large number of F-104s built, most parts are not too hard to obtain. Tires can be one of the more critical parts to obtain, because they typically only last about 15 landings. When your supply of tires is gone, you are looking at a $75,000 custom tire order from Goodyear. He says the F-104 is a fun aircraft to fly, with low-level performance still faster than the current fighters. He points out that Darryl Greenamyer's low-altitude speed record in the F-104 still stands. Keeping your speed up is key in flying the F-104.

Darryl Greenamyer's F-104

Darryl Greenamyer, a former Lockheed test pilot, built a flyable F-104 with a team of volunteers, by piecing together parts from military surplus scrap heaps and civilian junkyards. This project took 13 years and during construction picked up the nickname "Junkyard Jet." Effort was towards building an aircraft that could establish a new low-altitude world speed record. A water injection system was designed and installed on the engine that increased the mass flow through the core of the engine, which provided lower operating temperatures and increased the redline from Mach 2.3 to Mach 2.6.

Darryl Greenamyer's red and white finished project was called

Svetkoff's Starfighters, Inc. is an air show team based in Clearwater, Florida. The team currently has two F-104s, a single-place CF-104 and a two-place CF-104D. Here they are near the end of the runway ready for start prior to take-off at the EAA Sun and Fun show in Florida in April 1999. (Pete Clukey)

Starfighters Inc. CF-104, flown by Tom Delashaw and photographed by Pete Clukey, flying in the Starfighters, Inc CF-104D with Svetkoff on a flight from Pope AFB North Carolina to Clearwater Florida in July 2001. (Pete Clukey)

Rick Svetkoff, flying Starfighters, Inc. CF-104D, on landing approach at the April 2000 Knoxville air show. (Pete Clukey)

Darryl Greenamyer's Red Baron *F-104 at Mojave airport, California. Greenamyer flew his Starfighter to a Low Altitude World Speed Record of 988.260 miles per hour in October 1977. This was officially certified by the FAI on 31 January 1978.* (via Tony Landis)

the *Red Baron*, and carried the civil registration number N104RB. The low-altitude speed record runs were made at Mud Lake, a dry lake bed in Nevada. Elaborate timing devices were set up, and four runs were required. An observer described the *Red Baron*'s approach: "A small dot appeared on the horizon and then he was there, a strike of red and white slicing through the course 30 or 40 feet off the ground in eerie silence. A few seconds later, a shock wave like a cannon blast shattered the silence, but Darryl was already out of sight on a 15-mile loop to get into position for his second run." Greenamyer set a new Low Altitude World Speed Record of 988.260 miles per hour with the F-104 *Red Baron* on that day in October 1977. The record run was officially certified by the FAI on 31 January 1978.

After the speed record, the Red Baron was further modified with extended wing tips, reaction control components, and the longer nose of the NF-104A, borrowed from the static display at Edwards AFB. At the end of a full-up practice run for a new world's altitude record on 27 February 1978, the right main landing did not indicate down and locked and could not be verified as down and locked. Fuel was low, and handbook procedure was to eject in this situation, since a gear-up or one-gear-down landing was not considered survivable. Greenamyer successfully ejected and 13 years of work ended.

Civil Starfighters

There have been several interesting civil uses of the F-104, with NASA having the largest quantity (11), which they used for a total of 39 years, longer than any U.S. Air Force operation of the 104.

Specifications

A

The Numbers

	F-104A	F-104B	F-104C	F-104G	F-104S
Wing Span (feet & inches)	21′ 9″	21′ 9″	21′ 9″	21′ 9″	21′ 11″
Length (feet & inches)	54′ 8″	54′ 8″	54′ 8″	54′ 8″	54′ 9″
Height (feet & inches)	13′ 5″	13′ 5″	13′ 5″	13′ 5″	13′ 6″
Wing Area (square feet)	196.1	196.1	196.1	196.1	196.1
Empty Weight (pounds)	13,384	13,327	12,760	13,966	14,900
Maximum Weight (pounds)	25,840	24,912	27,853	29,038	31,000
Combat Weight (pounds)	17,988	17,812	19,470	20,640	21,690
Max. Speed at Altitude (mph @ feet)	1,037@50,000	1,145@65,000	1,150@50,000	1,146@50,000	1,450@36,000
Cruise Speed (mph)	519	516	510	510	610
Max. Rate of Climb (feet per minute)	60,395	64,500	54,000	48,000	55,000
Service Ceiling (feet)	64,795	64,795	58,000	50,000	58,000
Normal Range (miles)	730	460	850	1,080	1,550
Maximum Range (miles)	1,400	1,225	1,500	1,630	1,815

Both XF-104s in flight during flight test. Number one, USAF s/n 53-7786, has tip tanks installed. The XF-104s did not have the conical inlets. Both of these aircraft were built in Kelly Johnson's Skunk Works. (Lockheed, Dave Steinbacher collection)

Production List

Appendix B

Lockheed F-104 Serial Numbers

Model	Manufacturer	msn	USAF Serial Number	Notes
XF-104	Lockheed	1001	53-7786	Prototypes powered by XJ65-W-6 engine with 10,200 lbs thrust
XF-104	Lockheed	1002	53-7787	
YF-104A -1	Lockheed	1001 thru 1017	55-2955 thru 55-2971	Production prototypes, lengthened fuselage and 14,800-lb thrust engine and new inlets
F-104A -1	Lockheed	1018 thru 1024	56-730 thru 56-736	14,800-lb thrust, six-barrel 20mm cannon
F-104A -5	Lockheed	1025 thru 1035	56-737 thru 56-747	
F-104A -10	Lockheed	1036 thru 1051	56-748 thru 56-763	
F-104A –15	Lockheed	1052 thru 1076	56-764 thru 56-788	
F-104A –20	Lockheed	1077 thru 1113	56-789 thru 56-825	
F-104A –25	Lockheed	1114 thru 1165	56-826 thru 56-877	
F-104A –30	Lockheed	1166 thru 1170	56-878 thru 56-882	
NF-104A	Lockheed	———	———	(3) Modified from F-104A's with rocket booster as aerospace trainer
QF-104A	Lockheed	———	———	(24) Target drone conversions from YF-104As and F-104As
RF-104A	Lockheed	———	56-939 thru 56-956	Photo reconnaissance version ordered but cancelled.
F-104B –1	Lockheed	5000 thru 5005	56-3719 thru 56-3724	Two-seat version of F-104A
F-104B –5	Lockheed	5006 thru 5014	57-1294 thru 56-1302	
F-104B –10	Lockheed	5015 thru 5023	57-1303 thru 57-1311	
F-104B –15	Lockheed	5024 thru 5025	57-1312 thru 57-1313	
F-104C –5	Lockheed	1171 thru 1226	56-883 thru 56-938	Blown flaps, removable refuel probe
F-104C –10	Lockheed	1227 thru 1247	57-910 thru 57-930	
F-104D –5	Lockheed	5026 thru 6032	57-1314 thru 57-1320	Two-seat version of F-104C
F-104D –10	Lockheed	5033 thru 5040	57-1321 thru 57-1328	
F-104D -15	Lockheed	5041 thru 5046	57-1329 thru 57-1334	
F-104DJ	Lockheed/Mitsubishi	26-5001 thru 26-5009	——	F-104D version for Japanese ASDF
F-104F	Lockheed	5047 thru 5076	59-4994 thru 59-5023	Two-seat version of F-104D equipped to F-104G standards for West German Air Force
F-104G	Lockheed	4001 thru 4023	61-2601 thru 61- 2623	All-weather fighter-bomber version of F-104C "Super Starfighter"
F-104G	Lockheed	4067 thru 4084	62-12214 thru 12231	
F-104G	Lockheed	2011 thru 2016	63-13230 thru 13235	
F-104G	Lockheed	2018	63-13236	
F-104G	Lockheed	2020 thru 2028	63-13237 thru 13245	
F-104G	Lockheed	2030 thru 2042	63-13246 thru 13258	
F-104G	Lockheed	2010, 2076	63-13259 thru 13260	
F-104G	Lockheed	2069	67-14887	

F-104G	Messerschmitt	7001	65-12745	Germany
F-104G	Messerschmitt	7098,7035	65-12747, 65-12748	
F-104G	Messerschmitt	7120, 7132	66-13524, 66-13525	
F-104G	Messerschmitt	7177	66-13526	
F-104G	Messerschmitt	7133, 7023	67-14885, 67-14886	
F-104G	Messerschmitt	7007, 7015	67-14888, 67-14889	
F-104G	Fokker	8056	63-13229	Netherlands
F-104G	Fokker	8183, 8188	63-13690, 63-13691	
F-104G	Fokker	8021, 8064	65-12746, 65-12749	
F-104G	Fokker	8067, 8069	65-12750, 65-12752	
F-104G	Fokker	8071, 8077	65-12753, 65-12754	
F-104G	Fokker	8204, 8192	67-14890, 67-14892	
F-104G	Fokker	8230	67-22517	
F-104G	SABCA-Fairy	8196, 2086	63-13261, 63-13262	Belgium
F-104G	SABCA-Fairy	2091 thru 2095	63-13263 thru 63-13265	
F-104G	SABCA-Fairy	2095 thru 2097	63-13266 thru 63-13268	
F-104G	SABCA-Fairy	8002, 8003	63-13269, 63-13270	
F-104G	SABCA-Fairy	8007, 8009	63-13271 thru 13273	
F-104G	SABCA-Fairy	9001 thru 9005	63-13274 thru 63-13278	
F-104G	Canadair	6001 thru 6048	62-12302 thru 62-12349	MAP
F-104G	Canadair	6050 thru 6059	62-12698 thru 62-12707	MAP
F-104G	Canadair	6087 thru 6096	63-13628 thru 63-13647	MAP
F-104G	Canadair	6097 thru 6140	64-17752 thru 64-17795	MAP
CF-104	Canadair	——	Interceptor version	Canadian version of F-104G
CF-104D	Lockheed	———		Two-seat variant
RF-104G	Lockheed	4024 thru 4033	61-2624 thru 61-2633	Tactical reconnaissance version of the F-104G. Some had ventral camera pods
RF-104G	Lockheed	4034 thru 4044	62-12232 thru 62-12242	
RF-104G	Lockheed	4046 thru 4052	62-12243 thru 62-12249	
RF-104G	Lockheed	4054 thru 4057	62-12250 thru 62-12253	
RF-104G	Lockheed	4059 thru 4066	62-12254 thru 62-12261	
RF-104G	Fokker	8191	67-14891	
RF-104G	Fokker	8177	67-14893	
RF-104G	Lockheed	5501 thru 5506	61-3025 thru 61-3030	
TF-104G	Lockheed	5701	61-3031	Two-seat version of F-104G,
TF-104G	Lockheed	5703 thru 5755	61-3032 thru 61-3084	
TF-104G	Lockheed	5507 thru 5524	62-12262 thru 62-12279	
TF-104G	Lockheed	5756 thru 5766	63-8452 thru 63-8462	
TF-104G	Lockheed	5768	63-8463	
TF-104G	Lockheed	5770, 5771	63-8464, 63-8465	
TF-104G	Lockheed	5773, 5775	63-8466, 63-8467	
TF-104G	Lockheed	5777, 5779	63-8468, 63-8469	
TF-104G	Lockheed	5525 thru 5528	63-12681 thru 12684	
TF-104G	Lockheed	5767, 5769	63-12685, 63-12686	
TF-104G	Lockheed	5772, 5774	63-12687, 63-12688	
TF-104G	Lockheed	5776, 5778	63-12689, 63-12690	
TF-104G	Lockheed	5780 thru 5785	63-12691 thru 63-12696	
TF-104G	Lockheed	5786 thru 5788	64-15104 thru 64-15106	
TF-104G	Lockheed	5529	65-9415	
TF-104G	Lockheed	5933 thru 5942	66-13622 thru 13631	
F-104J	Lockheed	—	—	F-104G for Japanese ASDF
F-104J	Mitsubishi	—	———	Mitsubishi assembled 29 from Lockheed-supplied parts
F-104J	Mitsubishi	—	——	Mitsubishi built 177 F-104Js
F-104S	Lockheed	—	—	Two prototypes from F-104G
F-104S	Fiat-Aeritalia	—	—	245 built

MODEL KIT GUIDE

BY RICHARD MARMO

The F-104 Starfighter has definitely been well represented in the lists of model manufacturers in scales ranging all the way from a 1/110th scale kit by Comet (you've got to be at least 50 years old to remember seeing those on the shelves of five-and-dimes) to Hasegawa's 1/32nd effort. Companies such as Revell, Aurora, Lindberg, Monogram, Hasegawa, Airfix, Frog, Heller, Faller, Tamiya and many others have added F-104 kits to their lists. And just in case you've wondered why any manufacturer would add a new F-104 kit to their own catalog when there are many others already available, the answer is quite simple: Because *they* don't have one. It's called competition. Besides every manufacturer *knows* that their latest and greatest effort is going to be better than any other kit of the same subject that's already on the market ... even if it really isn't.

Quality ... and in some cases, accuracy ... was equally wide ranging. Some efforts were truly creative, such as the Monogram Airpower set produced in 1/240th scale that included models of every aircraft in the USAF inventory at the time. Each model was mounted on a wire rod that supported each model in flight position. While the scale was quite small, the finished product made for an impressive and educational display.

If an attempt was made to list every F-104 plastic kit that's been produced since the late 1950s, there wouldn't be enough room on two pages to do it. Include the same kit that's been repopped by nine different manufacturers and it gets even worse. Besides, many of these kits are so obscure that they're known only to collectors and rare as hen's teeth besides. To that end, only those that are generally available at this time or can be tracked down with relatively little trouble have been included here.

Appearing originally in the 1957 Revell catalog, this (PN H-142) was probably the best of the early F-104 kits.

Revell of Germany frequently offers kits (like this one, PN 04344) that are not released in the U.S.

Revell (H-142) F-104A. This kit appeared in the late 1950s and probably deserves credit for popularizing the F-104 with modelers. Produced with the full co-operation of the USAF and Lockheed, it was as accurate as it could be when you consider that some aspects of the design were still secret. Scale was 1/64th to fit the box and quality was state of the art for the time period. Price? 89 cents in 1957. You'll need to deal with a collector to get this one.

Between reissues that change nothing but the markings, repops

Unable to settle on an early or late version? This later Revell kit (PN H-236) includes two complete tail sections so it's easier to decide.

using molds from defunct companies and reciprocal marketing agreements, it's a full-time job and then some to keep track of who's using whose molds and when. It can also become somewhat of a guessing game as to what kind of surface detail (recessed panel lines or raised, etc.) you should expect, level of quality and so on. Obviously, that's more of a problem with some companies than it is others.

When is an F-104 not an F-104? When it's an F-104G, which is what this Monogram kit (PN 5409) is, in spite of the boxtop designation.

The following list of F-104 kits either are or have been commonly available in hobby shops, mail order shops or other catalogs since somewhere around the mid-1990s to the present time. Quality ranges from good to excellent. By the time you read this, there will probably be several – if not many – more.

Italeri (IT1223) F-104G, 1/72nd scale.

Italeri (IT01234) F-104A/C, 1/72nd scale, USAF markings. As this is written, this latest release from Italeri has just been announced. Because of the greater number of countries (and the equally greater diversity in markings), the later F-104G/J variant tends to be more popular with manufacturers. Anyone interested in the early USAF version should welcome this latest Italeri effort with open arms.

Hasegawa (00447) F-104G, 1/72 scale.

Hasegawa (HE07220) F-104G, 1/48th scale, NATO markings.

Hasegawa (various kit numbers) F-104G/J, 1/32 scale. This was the original large scale F-104. Produced in the late 1970s, it was a superb effort. Despite the change to engraved panel lines on most current models versus raised lines on this kit, it would still qualify as one of the best F-104 kits ever produced.

Hasegawa (HE08133) F-104C, 1/32nd scale, 479th TFW markings.

Revell of Germany (04344) F-104G, 1/72nd scale, German Air Force markings.

Revell of Germany (04302) F-104C, 1/72nd scale, USAF markings

Revell (H236) F-104C/G, 1/48th scale, USAF or German markings. This 2-in-1 kit provides two separate aft fuselage/vertical tail sections that allow you to create either an early or late F-104.

Monogram (5409) F-104, 1/48th scale, USAF, German, Netherlands or Canadian markings. The boxtop says that this only an "F-104," but it's actually a very nice F-104G.

Hawk (various kit numbers) F-104, 1/48th scale, USAF markings. Originally produced in both bare styrene and chrome plated, this kit has been repopped time and again by both Hawk and it's successor, Testors.

Testors (7523) F-104C, 1/48th scale, USAF markings. The latest non-plated incarnation of the original Hawk kit, it's available as part of Testors HSO (Hobby Shop Only) line.

While there's no way it can compete with the latest state of the art kits, it looks like an F-104, is an easy build and costs a lot less than many of the kits on the market today. If you're just getting into model building, or returning after a long hiatus, this kit's a good starter choice.

This HSO kit's been around for decades, but it's still a creditable kit.

Significant Dates

Key Dates in the History of the Lockheed F-104 Starfighter

1951
Kelly Johnson travels to Korea to find out what the pilots need in a fighter.

October 1951
Lockheed preliminary design begins for a new fighter that would fly higher and faster than any fighter of the time.

31 October 1952
Lockheed management approves preliminary design number CL-246 for the new fighter.

December 1952
A briefing on the new design is held at Wright Patterson Field.

December 1952
Kelly Johnson presents the new fighter design at the Pentagon.

March 1953
USAF awards a contract to Lockheed to build two XF-104s.

4 March 1954
The XF-104 is flown for the first time by Lockheed test pilot Tony LeVier.

25 March 1955
Lockheed test pilot Ray Goudey achieves a speed of Mach 1.79 on the XF-104 during a test flight — the highest speed on the J65 powered prototype.

17 February 1956
The YF-104A production prototype flies for the first time, powered by the General Electric J79.

27 April 1956
YF-104 reaches Mach 2.

29 January 1958
The first operational F-104A is delivered to Hamilton Air Force Base, California.

7 May 1958
A world altitude record of 91,249 feet is set by Major Howard C. Johnson at Edwards AFB in the F-104A.

16 May 1958
Captain Walter W. Irwin sets a new world airspeed record of 1,404m mph over a 15/25 km course at Edwards AFB. The F-104 becomes the first aircraft to hold World Airspeed and Altitude records simultaneously.

15 October 1958
The USAF accepts the first F-104C at George Air Force Base, California.

November 1958
The first Operational F-104D accepted at George Air Force Base, California.

Late 1958
Two squadrons of USAF F-104As from Hamilton AFB go into action for the first time from National Chinese and American bases on Taiwan.

18 December 1958
The F-104A sets three time-to-climb records at NAS Point Mugu, California.: 3000 meters in 41.35 seconds; 15,000 meters in 2 minutes 11.1 seconds; and 25,000 meters (82,020 feet) in 4 minutes 26.03 seconds.

1959
Kelly Johnson receives the Collier Trophy for his design work on the F-104.

14 December 1959
Captain Joe Jordan, flying an F-104C at Edwards AFB, sets a new altitude record of 103,389 feet, reaching 1400 mph and establishing a 30,000-meter time-to-climb record of 5 minutes 4.92 seconds.

7 June 1960
First flight of the F-104G.

1 November 1961
Three US Air National Guard F-104 fighter interceptor squadrons are activated for deployment to Europe during the Berlin Crisis.

1962
USAF F-104Cs are deployed to bases in the southeastern United States during the Cuban missile crisis to counter the threat of Soviet-supplied MiG fighters operating from that island.

1963
Jacqueline Cochran sets the women's world speed records in the Lockheed TF-104G Super Starfighter: 1273.1 mph 12 April 1963 on a 15/25 km Straightaway Course and 1203.68 mph on a 100 km Closed Course on 1 May 1963.

6 December 1963
An NF-104A flown by Major Robert W. Smith sets an unofficial height record of 118, 860 feet for aircraft taking off on its own power.

March 1965
USAF F-104Cs head to South Vietnam to counter North Vietnamese interference with USAF strike aircraft.

December 1966
The F-104S, designed for the Italian Air Force, flies for the first time.

October 1977
Darryl Greenamyer sets a low-altitude world speed record of 988.260 mph with his modified F-104.

March 1979
The last Starfighter to be produced, an F-104S, rolls off the line in Italy.

December 1984
A modernized F-104S ASA makes its first flight in Italy.

March 1986
The last CF-104s are phased out of Canadian service.

November 2002
Alenia finishes upgrading the Italian F-104S to the F-104S ASAM configuration intended to keep it in operation until it is replaced by the Typhoon.

MORE GREAT TITLES FROM SPECIALTY PRESS

KILLER RAYS: The Story of the Douglas F4D Skyray & F5D Skylancer

The definitive work on the history of the Navy's only operational delta-wing aircraft. 8-1/2 x 11, 240 pgs, 50 color & 350 b/w photos plus 25 illustrations. Hdbd.
Item # SP155

FROM PROPS TO JETS: Commercial Aviation's Transition to the Jet Age 1952–1962

An in-depth look at all the aircraft that made commercial jet fight possible. 8-1/2 x 11, 160 pgs, 120 bw & 60 color photos, 20 illustrations. Hdbd.
Item # SP146

HELICOPTER GUNSHIPS: Deadly Combat Weapon Systems

Begins with gunships from the Vietnam War and goes through post-war programs like the Cheyenne, Blackhawk, and Apache. 8-1/2 x 11, 208 pgs, 100 b/w & 200 color photos, plus 20 illustrations. Hdbd.
Item # SP154

COLD WAR PEACEMAKER: The Story of Cowtown and Convair's B-36

Story of this plane's tech aspects and the political and social events that lead to its development in Fort Worth Texas. 8-1/2 x 11, 228 pgs, 300 b/w photos with 20 illustrations. Hdbd.
Item # SP127

AMARG: America's Military Aircraft Boneyard

Detail coverage of the famed storage and salvage facility in Tucson. Aerial and ground photos plus a comprehensive listing of all aircraft types currently at AMARG. 11 x 8-1/2, 144 pgs, 50 b/w & 350 color photos. Sftbd.
Item # SP139

CONVAIR ADVANCED DESIGNS: Secret Projects from San Diego, 1923-1962

Futuristic, stillborn concepts brought to life with company photos, models and drawings. 8-1/2 x 11, 192 pgs, 325 b/w photos & illus. Hdbd.
Item # SP133

U.S. AIR FORCE INTERCEPTORS: A Military Photo Logbook 1946–1979

Photo compilation of all of the great USAF Air Defense Command interceptors from the entire Cold War era. 8.5 x 11, 120 pgs, 150 b/w & 150 color photos. Sftbd.
Item # SP150

Birds of Prey: Predators, Reapers and America's Newest UAVs in Combat

History and development of unmanned aerial vehicles. 8-1/2 x 11, 160 pgs, 100 b/w & 200 color photos. Sftbd.
Item # SP153

CONVAIR DELTAS: From SeaDart to Hustler

Noted aviation author Bill Yenne thoroughly documents Convair's quest to conquer the aerodynamic mysteries of the delta wing with stories of the dramatic struggles and technological breakthroughs that gave the world some of its greatest fighter and bomber aircraft. 9 x 9, 216 pgs, 200 b/w & 130 color photos with 44 illustrations. Hdbd.
Item # SP118

LOCKHEED BLACKBIRD FAMILY: A-12, YF-12, D-21/M-21 & SR-71 Photo Scrapbook

Considered by many the world's most popular and most exciting aircraft, this edition includes many never-before-published photos coupled with new de-classified information recently released by the CIA, including black-and-white and color photos of A-12 cockpits, early camera installations, and never-before-seen special camouflage schemes. 8-1/2 x 11, 128 pgs, 425 illustrations. Sftbd.
Item # SP151

FIRE BOMBERS IN ACTION VIDEOBOOK

This book takes the reader inside the gritty world of aerial firefighting using both still photographs and dramatic video footage of these amazing aircraft and the men who fly them. Covering more than four decades of study and exposure to aerial firefighting in many regions of the United States, this book tells the story from the earliest attempts to combat dangerous and sometimes deadly wildfires with the use of aircraft. 8-1/2 x 11, 160 pgs, 150 b/w & 150 color photos. Sftbd.
Item # SP147

SP123 **Gunships:** The Story of Spooky, Shadow, Stinger and Spectre
SP149 **History of the Liberty Engine:** Tanks, Ships & A/C 1917-60
SP145 **Grumman F9F Panther/ Cougar:** First Grumman Cat of the Jet Age
SP138 **Servicing the Hubble Space Telescope:** Shuttle Atlantis 2009
SP137 **USAF Prototype Jet Fighters Scrapbook**
SP136 **MiG Killers:** Chronology of Vietnam Victories
SP132 **Strike From the Sea**
SP131 **Hypersonic:** Story of the NA X-15
SP129 **Magnesium Overcast:** Story of the Convair B-36
SP125 **American Secret Pusher Fighters of WWII:** XP-54, XP-55, XP-56
SP124 **North American's T-6**
SP122 **Northrop's Night Hunter:** P-61 Black Widow
SP121 **X-Plane Crashes:** Incidents, Accidents, & Crash Sites
SP119 **Clear the Deck!:** Carrier Accidents from WWII
SP116 **Radical Wings & Wind Tunnels:** Adv Concepts Tested at Langley
SP114 **U.S. Naval Aviation, Volume 1**
SP113 **U.S. Air Force Aviation, Volume 1**
SP111 **Experimental & Prototype U.S. Air Force Jet Fighters**
SP110 **U.S. Naval Air Superiority:** Jet Fighters 1943-1962
SP109 **U.S. Experimental & Prototype Aircraft Projects:** Fighters 1939-1945
SP099 **F-117 Nighthawk Photo Scrapbook**
SP092 **Strike and Return:** US Air Power & the Fight for Iwo Jima
SP087 **Stearman Aircraft**
SP084 **Skystreak, Skyrocket, & Stiletto:** Douglas High-Speed X-Planes
SP076 **X-Planes Photo Scrapbook**
SP064 **How to Build Sci-Fi Model Spacecraft**
SP097P **R-4360: Pratt & Whitney's Major Miracle**

AIRLINERTECH SERIES

SP017P **Douglas DC-6 & DC-7:** ALT Vol. 4
SP026P **Boeing 747 100/200/300:** ALT Vol. 6
SP037P **Lockheed L1011 TriStar:** ALT Vol. 8
SP047P **Boeing 377 Stratocruiser:** ALT Vol. 9

RACEPLANETECH SERIES

SP034P **Griffon-Powered Mustangs:** RPT Vol. 1
SP035P **Round Engine Racers Bearcats & Corsairs:** RPT Vol. 2

WARBIRDTECH SERIES

SP479P **Boeing B-29 Superfortress:** WBT Vol. 14
SP019P **Convair B-36 Peacemaker:** WBT Vol. 24
SP029P **Martin B-26 Marauder:** WBT Vol. 29
SP056P **North American Valkyrie XB-70:** WBT Vol. 34
SP069P **Lockheed F-104 Starfighter:** WBT Vol. 38
SP085 **MiG-29 Fulcrum:** WBT Vol. 41
SP091 **Sukhoi Su-27 Flanker:** WBT Vol. 42
SP102 **Tupolev Tu-95 Bear:** WBT Vol. 43

Specialty Press

39966 Grand Ave., North Branch, MN 55056
Fax (651) 277-1203 Phone 1-800-895-4585 www.specialtypress.com

Lightning Source UK Ltd.
Milton Keynes UK
UKOW01f2137281213

223643UK00004B/128/P

9 781580 071871